THE PRACTICAL
DRUCKER

Applying the Wisdom of the World's
Greatest Management Thinker

William A. Cohen

AMACOM

AMERICAN MANAGEMENT ASSOCIATION

New York • Atlanta • Brussels • Chicago • Mexico City • San Francisco
Shanghai • Tokyo • Toronto • Washington, D.C.

Bulk discounts available. For details visit:
www.amacombooks.org/go/specialsales
Or contact special sales:
Phone: 800-250-5308
Email: specialsls@amanet.org
View all the AMACOM titles at: www.amacombooks.org
American Management Association: www.amanet.org

Library of Congress Cataloging-in-Publication Data

Cohen, William A., 1937–
    The practical Drucker : applying the wisdom of the world's greatest management thinker / William A. Cohen.
        pages cm
    Includes index.
    ISBN-13: 978-0-8144-3349-2 (hardcover)
    ISBN-10: 0-8144-3349-9 (hardcover)
1. Drucker, Peter F. (Peter Ferdinand), 1909–2005. 2. Management. I. Title.
    HD31.D776C64 2013
    658--dc23   2013022526

About AMA

American Management Association (www.amanet.org) is a world leader in talent development, advancing the skills of individuals to drive business success. Our mission is to support the goals of individuals and organizations through a complete range of products and services, including classroom and virtual seminars, webcasts, webinars, podcasts, conferences, corporate and government solutions, business books, and research. AMA's approach to improving performance combines experiential learning—learning through doing—with opportunities for ongoing professional growth at every step of one's career journey.

Printing number
10 9 8 7 6 5 4 3 2

CONTENTS

Part Two | Management

Part Three | Marketing and Innovation

Part Four | Organizaton

FOREWORD

I must confess that my first reaction when I learned of the title of Bill Cohen's new book, *The Practical Drucker,* was to think to myself: "Hmmm. Perhaps an official from the Department of Redundancy Department should be asked to write the foreword instead."

In my mind, after all, Drucker and practicality are synonymous. Calling a book *The Practical Drucker* is like referring to someone as a "big giant" or a 100-story building as a "tall skyscraper."

Indeed, Drucker was so practical that much of the scholarly community regarded him as a pariah. Although he taught at four institutions of higher learning over his long career—Sarah Lawrence College, Bennington College, New York University, and Claremont Graduate University—Drucker never fit the mold of many of his colleagues. Those around him often seemed most interested in racking up citations in peer-reviewed academic journals; Drucker, for his part, was focused on making a difference in the real world.

"Being incomprehensible has become a virtue in academia," Drucker complained in the mid-1980s. By contrast, he added, "I have a deep horror of obscurity and arrogance"—a trait that constantly pushed him to present his work "in a form that people could apply."

He hardly used footnotes. He eschewed regression analysis, charts, and graphs. As a consultant to major corporations and non-profits, he stressed the need to put ideas into action. "Don't tell me you had a wonderful meeting with me," he'd say. "Tell me what you're going to do on Monday that's different."

Theory was fine with Drucker, but only insofar as it helped to lead to pragmatic solutions to pressing issues. "Sure, we want and need research," he said. "But consider the modern medical school, which began in the late 18th century. The emphasis in medical school is not on publication but on the ability to treat patients and make a difference in their lives." In a similar manner, he believed, "business educators should be out as practitioners where the problems and results are."

This fundamental insight—that writing about management and leadership isn't worth a whole lot if it isn't rooted in the day-to-day trials of organizational life—lies at the heart of Drucker's work. It is also where many of his peers get things backward.

"Intellectuals and scholars tend to believe that ideas come first, which then lead to new political, social, economic, psychological realities," Drucker wrote. "This does happen, but it is the exception. As a rule, theory does not precede practice. Its role is to structure and codify already proven practice. Its role is to convert the isolated and 'atypical' from exception to 'rule' and 'system,' and therefore into something that can be learned and taught and, above all, into something that can be generally applied."

This bent toward application, toward action, toward usefulness, animated everything that Drucker did. In the end, it was what set him apart. Drucker "spoke in plain language that resonated with ordinary managers," Andy Grove, the co-founder of Intel, has remarked. "Consequently, simple statements from him have influenced untold numbers of daily actions; they did mine over decades."

Tom Peters, the best-selling management writer who also bends strongly toward the practical, once praised Drucker for his pioneering role in helping "incredibly complex organizations" run better. "Drucker was the first person to give us a handbook for that," he said.

Actually, that's not quite right. Rather than produce one handbook, Drucker penned thirty-nine books and thousands of articles over many decades—a trove so immense that, all in all, it may add up to the most impractical thing he ever did.

How many times have you ever thought, "What would Drucker say?" about a particular situation—and then tried to quickly find the answer? Where do you begin? Perhaps *The Practice of Management* is the best source. But what about *Managing for Results*? No, wait. Maybe what you really need is a later text, like *Management Challenges for the 21st Century*. Searching through this vast ocean of content when all you want to take away is a single glass of water can be difficult, if not downright frustrating.

Drucker's output was so massive, it led another best-selling management writer, Jim Collins, to ask a pointed question. Although Collins is a huge Drucker fan, he couldn't help but wonder, "Do you think Peter Drucker would have been more influential if he had written less?"

I'd argue no, but I get the point. And this is where Bill Cohen's book comes in. By combing through Drucker's enormous body of work and deftly synthesizing the "how to do" (as opposed to the "what to do") aspects of his writing, Bill has made a great contribution. In this way, *The Practical Drucker* is less redundant and more a revelation.

"Knowledgeable executives are plentiful," Drucker observed shortly before he passed away in 2005. "But executives are not being paid for knowing. They are being paid for getting the right things done." *The Practical Drucker* is a terrific road map for achieving this all-important end.

Rick Wartzman
Executive Director, The Drucker Institute

INTRODUCTION

Some six years ago, I was at the Rosario University in Bogotá, Colombia, at the invitation of the faculty and administration to speak about Peter Drucker. The ancient Universidad del Rosario (which is its official name in Spanish) was founded in 1653 by Roman Catholic clergy and scholars under the authorization of King Philip IV of Spain. Harvard, the first U.S. college, is older (1636), but not by much. Nowadays, Rosario University is far more secular and holds an important place in Colombian history, such that it is known as "The Cradle of the Republic." Twenty-eight of Colombia's presidents have been its students. Some say a few more probably attended before accurate records started being kept. I was honored to be invited to speak at such an illustrious institution.

A Spanish translation of my book *A Class with Drucker* had recently been published in Bogotá. There was some buzz, since Peter Drucker's business genius was receiving great attention in Colombia, as it was in many other countries. In addition to my speaking in the morning, I was to join my colleague Dr. Joe Maciariello, from the Peter F. Drucker and Masatoshi Graduate School of Management at California's Claremont Graduate University, on a panel to discuss Drucker's teachings. One senior executive on that panel had read my book; he commented that while he had read many of Drucker's books, what struck him as different about mine was how much easier it made it to apply Drucker's concepts. I thanked him and suggested that this might have to do with some peculiarities of translation into Spanish, but that I was happy to take the credit and was going to quote him to my wife as soon as possible.

After some reflection, I began to understand what he meant. It wasn't that Drucker wrote poorly. On the contrary, Drucker made his living from his writings for general interest magazines long before he became a consultant. Nor was it that Drucker wasn't specific about what he wrote. Indeed, Drucker was very specific in both his speeches and his writings. However, while Drucker was definitely application-oriented, rather than theoretically oriented, he focused on what to do but he rarely wrote about how to do it.

In his consulting work, Drucker apparently did even less explaining. One of his clients described to me how difficult it was to understand Drucker: "Unlike other consultants, he didn't tell us either what to do or how to do it. Rather, he asked us questions that we were supposed to answer." He went on to explain: "Eventually we realized how effective this technique was and the genius behind it. He made us grasp his ideas on our own. This was far more helpful in our applying them; however, it was slow going at first, and doing this based on his writings was sometimes even more difficult."

My first stab at professional writing involved my Air Force specialty of navigation. The intention was to write for navigation journals, providing clear instructions that could be read and understood in several different countries. This simple goal in writing has been carried forward to my books on business, management, and strategy. That is, "how-to-do-it" discussions are usually easier to comprehend than "what-to-do" discussions. So, for better or worse, this is what you will find in *The Practical Drucker*.

Drucker's powerful observations about people and the organizations in which they worked sometimes took the form of deceptively simple truths and astute predictions. Concepts such as decentralization, outsourcing, the rise of the knowledge worker, viewing employees as assets, a focus on the customer, marketing as different from selling—it was Peter Drucker who first expressed every one of these ideas, sometimes decades before they became the accepted wisdom they are today. In the same way, he predicted our current financial challenges years before they occurred.

What I have done in *The Practical Drucker* is to mine Drucker's vast body of work to explain forty of his most important concepts and truths: keys for solving real-world problems and fundaments for today's effective management and keen leadership. However, I have carried his ideas a step further: I explain not only what needs to be done to implement his concepts but also how to go about *doing* this implementation. If there are mistakes here, they are mine. The genius is pure Drucker.

PART ONE

1

People

CHAPTER ONE

General Business Ethics

Peter Drucker was extremely ethical in his outlook as well as in his actions. On a personal level, he was one of the most principled individuals I have ever met. From both his writing and his classroom lectures, it was clear that he sought to arrive at basic ethical principles that were essential for business. He believed that ethical behavior was an absolute requirement of all organizational leaders, that they should incorporate integrity and ethics into how they conducted their business. First and foremost, he concluded that while followers would forgive an organizational leader much, they would not forgive a lack of integrity in personal dealings. However, Drucker well understood that interpretations of ethics and integrity might vary and therefore it was not easy trying to derive a common point of ethics that would be applicable as general business ethics.

Drucker Investigates Business Ethics

As he grappled mightily to understand ethics, Peter Drucker cast a wide net, beginning with ethical philosophies from the Western tradition and expanding his search both geographically and historically.

He did find a single point of complete agreement, and one point only, in which an ethical code of sorts applied universally. (More about that later.) There were usually various types of extenuating circumstances within all ethical interpretations. For example, clemency might be granted to someone who violates a code of ethics under certain circumstances. "Thou shalt not steal" is one of the Ten Commandments. Yet a mother stealing to feed a starving child might be excused as committing a lesser evil for a greater good. Differences in ethics owing to differences in social or cultural mores might also be accepted.

Javier Bardem won an Academy Award for Best Supporting Actor for his role as the villain and killer Anton Chigurh in the movie *No Country for Old Men*. Asked who Chigurh was, Woody Harrelson's character, Carson Welles, responded: "Anton is a man of principle. But he just doesn't follow the same principles that you and I might agree should be followed."

In fact, practices of questionable morality by one individual, or a group of individuals, might not only be considered acceptable but also quite ethical.[1] For example, extremists who willingly blow themselves and innocent bystanders up with explosives for their radical version of Islam consider their actions to be ethical, while others might vigorously disagree.

But what about doing things in business that are clearly "unethical"? Can business ethics be defined in this manner? This came up in Drucker's class, and I also found his response in one of his books: "Hiring call girls to entertain visiting executives does not make you unethical. It merely makes you a pimp."[2] This brought general laughter in class, but it was clearly representative of Drucker's limitations of business ethics.

Extortion or Bribery

Drucker noted that bribery was hardly desirable from the viewpoint of the victim who was being extorted. It had been made illegal for U.S. companies through a law prohibiting the payment of bribes to obtain foreign contracts. This bribery was cited as a gross violation of "business ethics."

But Drucker was very clear on this. He thought it was stupid to pay bribes. However, was paying bribes in itself a violation of the law or of business ethics? Most countries have laws against bribery. Yet it is a fact that bribery, as we define it, is routine and expected in some of these countries. Several of the countries recognize "baksheesh" as the traditional way of doing business. Their citizens may ignore any local laws that have been enacted, regarding them as "window dressing" and not part of their own culture.

Drucker noted in his investigation that a private citizen who was extorted into paying a bribe to a criminal might be considered foolish or a helpless victim of intimidation. And certainly paying extortion is never desirable. But this was clearly not an ethical issue on the part of the individual who might be forced to face a greater ethical threat, not to himself, but to members of his family or the general public. He objected to any "new business ethics" that might assert that acts not immoral or illegal if done by private citizens would become immoral or illegal if done in the context of a business organization without examining the circumstances. They might be stupid, they might be illegal, and they might be the wrong thing to do. However, they do not necessarily constitute "business ethics."

The Ethics of Social Responsibility

Drucker looked closely at casuistry, or rationalization. Casuistry might also be termed cost-benefit ethics, or ethics for the greater good. Essentially it says that someone in power, such as a CEO, a king, or a president, has a higher duty if it can be argued that his behavior confers benefits on others. So, it is wrong to lie, but in the interests of "the country" or "the company," or "the organization," it sometimes has to be done. Drucker maintained that this was too dangerous a concept to be adopted as business ethics because a business leader could use it to justify what would clearly be unethical behavior for anyone else.[3] Drucker looked further.

The Ethics of Prudence

To be prudent means to be careful or cautious. It is a rather unusual philosophy for an ethical approach, but admittedly it has some benefits.

Drucker gave an example of prudence that pertains to senior military officers. He said that Harry Truman, at the time a U.S. senator, gave this advice to a general officer witness before his committee in the early years of World War II: "Generals should never do anything that needs to be explained to a Senate Committee—there is nothing one can explain to a Senate Committee."[4]

He thought that Truman's advice may be pretty good for staying out of trouble, but it was not much of a basis for ethical business decision making. For one thing, it doesn't tell a person anything about what the right kind of behavior is. For another, there are decisions that a leader must make that are risky and that may be difficult to explain, especially if things go wrong—but they may nevertheless be the correct decisions to make.

The Ethics of Profit

Though he called it "The Ethics of Profit," it is not what you might think. Drucker did not say anything about limiting profits. Much to the contrary, he wrote that it would be socially irresponsible, and most certainly unethical, if a business did *not* show a profit at least equal to the cost of capital, because failing to do so would waste society's resources.[5] However, the only logical rationale for the justification of "profit" was that it was a cost. His advice was as follows: "Check to see if you are earning enough profit to cover the cost of capital and provide for innovation. If not, what are you going to do about it?"[6]

Although he died just days short of his ninety-sixth birthday in 2005, two years before the onset of the recession he had predicted years earlier, Drucker would have supported those companies defending their profits as necessary for marketing and innovation, two essential (and ethical, Drucker implied) requirements for any business. For, while profit was an ethical goal, its use as a "metric" rested on very weak moral grounds, and as an ethical incentive it could be justified only if it were a genuine cost, especially if this cost was required to maintain jobs and to grow new ones.[7]

Confucian Ethics

Calling Confucian ethics "the most successful and most durable of them all," Drucker looked to the East for guidance. He maintained an interest in Japan and China, which perhaps explains why the latter was the only country where he allowed an educational institution outside the United States (the Peter F. Drucker Academies of China and Hong Kong) to use his name. In Confucian ethics, the rules are the same for everyone, but there are different general rules that vary according to five basic relationships, all based on interdependence. These five relationships are:

1. Superior and subordinate

2. Father and child

3. Husband and wife

4. Oldest brother and sibling

5. Friend and friend

The "right" behavior in each case differs, so as to optimize benefits to both parties in the relationship. In essence, all have mutual obligations. This concept is not compatible with what is considered business ethics in many countries, including the United States, where one side has obligations and the other side in addition has rights and entitlements.

Though he clearly admired Confucian ethics, which he called "The Ethics of Interdependence," he concluded that its principles cannot be applied as business ethics because the Confucian system deals with matters between individuals, not between groups.[8]

A "Common Point" for Business Ethics

Primum non nocere is Latin for "above all, do no harm." It was part of the ancient physician Hippocrates's writings, but it is not the Hippocratic Oath as many (including Drucker) believed.[9] This simple phrase, Drucker thought, should be the basis of all notions of business ethics, though he did have other corollary conclusions based on his in-depth analysis. So his ethics struggles were not in vain. He concluded that business ethics as we know them today are not that at all. If ever business ethics were to be codified, he felt, they ought to be based on Confucian ethics, focusing on the *right* behavior rather than on misbehaviors or wrongdoings. In the meantime, organizational executives and practitioners should understand the following things about business ethics:[10]

1. There are many different approaches to ethics; none of them are 100 percent compatible with what we really should consider business ethics.

2. Confucian ethics—that is, the Ethics of Interdependence—probably comes closest to the ideal for what might be called organizational ethics.

3. The ethics of personal responsibility from the physician Hippocrates, "above all (or first), do no harm," is a good basis for business ethics.

4. The mirror test is not bad: "What kind of person do I want to see when I look into the mirror every morning?"

CHAPTER TWO

Drucker on Engagement

Some years ago, the author of a highly successful business book asked me whether I was interested in co-authoring a book he was working on about engagement. He wanted to tap into my experience as an Air Force general and use a play on words regarding the "rules of engagement" in the book's title.

"Rules of Engagement" has been adopted frequently as a term to describe the regulations under which a particular conflict is to be conducted. In the old days, there were prenegotiated "rules of warfare," such as those codified under the Hague Convention beginning in 1899. These rules required, among other tenets, that prisoners of war not be mistreated, that someone waving a white flag must be allowed to surrender, and that noncombatants or civilians not be intentionally targeted. However, the complexities of modern combat, politics, and the introduction of advanced technology such as aircraft, both piloted and pilotless, and missiles made new policies advisable. As a result, one side or the other might impose even more stringent rules on its own armies.

Thus, in the Vietnam War, U.S. pilots were prohibited from firing into a village from which they were being fired on, except under very specific circumstances—something that would have been considered ridiculous by the "Greatest Generation" who fought World War II. For people whose lives were at risk, this engagement rule seemed not very appreciative of the danger they faced and the fact that this was serious stuff. In any case, I decided that my being a retired general was insufficient reason to co-author a book. However, the experience served to confirm that the word *engagement* can have more than its surface meaning.

Business Engagement Is Also Serious Stuff

Use of the term "engagement" in business is fairly recent, only dating to business literature from the 1990s, when Frank L. Schmidt, then a senior scientist with the Gallup Organization, began to study the topic. He applied his unique statistical methodology and published his results in the academic literature, using this terminology.[1]

Whatever it was called, Drucker recognized its importance long before it was identified, and he showed how managers could develop it in their workforce. There was no doubt that to contribute significantly to the goals set by the manager, a fully engaged worker was required. The goal and outcome could not be merely performance; they had to be *outstanding* performance. The difference between performance and outstanding performance is like that between sports participation and an Olympic athlete. It is the difference between amateur acting and an acting performance that approaches Oscar quality.

Drucker said that to attain this level of output, the manager must create what he called "a responsible worker." Drucker expected an awful lot from the "responsible worker." The term "engaged worker" seems to be a better description. An engaged worker is one who is committed to contributing to the organization and is willing to exert extraordinary effort in accomplishing tasks important to the achievement of organizational goals. It's no small thing. Every study of engaged employees shows magnitudes of difference in performance between those who are engaged and those who are not.

Satisfaction Does Not Create an Engaged Worker

At one time or another, almost every organization conducts surveys to determine what has been described as "employee satisfaction." I once spoke on leadership to a large fifty-year-old organization and learned that this organization was in the midst of one of these satisfaction studies. Are these surveys useful? Maybe. They do represent an opportunity for employees to vent their irritants. They give leaders a feel for the major concerns in their organizations at that particular time. They may provide guidance for management decisions. However, as Drucker noted, they have their limitations.

"Employee satisfaction" is not easily defined and cannot be usefully quantified. For example, one cannot say that the fact that 75 percent of employees are satisfied is good, bad, or irrelevant. Even if a preponderance of workers agrees that this organization is a good place to work, that doesn't say much. I have seen satisfaction/dissatisfaction studies misused and so worded as to result in desired responses that then lead to predetermined courses of action.

Drucker's biggest criticism was that "satisfaction" or "dissatisfaction" responses simply aren't adequate and do not result in employee engagement. Even if compensation were an issue, a manager could buy personal responsibility with financial rewards only in a limited way or for a fixed period of time. Therefore, satisfaction alone cannot have a positive impact on generating real personal responsibility or creating an engaged employee. Drucker concluded that even a worker's *dissatisfaction* with some aspect of his work was far more likely to accomplish this, should he be empowered to initiate action to improve the situation and it caused him to do so. Drucker not only called satisfaction inadequate, he christened it "passive acquiescence."[2] That's also when he came up with the term "responsible worker." Peter expected a lot.

Drucker's Four Paths to an Engaged Worker

If satisfaction isn't key to creating the engaged worker, what is? Although I have seen dozens of methods that promise to result in engaged employees, Drucker found only four, and he stressed that these weren't alternative approaches, but that all four must be used simultaneously to achieve the desired results. These were:[3]

1. Aiming for careful placement and promotion

2. Demanding high standards of performance

3. Providing workers with information

4. Encouraging workers to acquire managerial vision

    Let's take a look at each of these.

Aiming for Careful Placement and Promotion

A systematic, serious, and continual effort to put people in the right jobs is a prerequisite for worker engagement, according to Drucker. Frequently, promotions are made with little discussion or any attempt at soliciting the opinion of other managers. Drucker very much admired the promotion system in the U.S. military, with its formal evaluations emphasizing performance, review, and fairness, and its promotion by a board rather than a single individual. In many cases, promotion made the selectee eligible for further assignment, which was also based on accumulated experience and performance over time. I think he saw this as akin to the system of management by objectives that he developed and taught.

Demanding High Standards of Performance

Adequate performance is generally associated with easy, low-demand work. For engagement, workers need to be challenged with much more. They need high standards of performance that will challenge their abilities. When I was his student, University of Chicago professor Thomas Whistler once described what happened to one of his most brilliant and capable doctoral students. The student had taken his first job after receiving his doctorate at a major corporation, but it was in a relatively low position. This gifted student apparently failed to perform to expectations and, recognizing this himself, he resigned. The former student then went to another corporation where he immediately did so well that within six months he was elevated to the position of vice president.

"The problem," Professor Whistler said, "was not that the first job was too big, but that it was too small. The mistake my former student made was to accept that job in the first place. My student had this amount of ability [Whistler raised his hand far above his head] and that first job required this amount [Whistler lowered his hand to about his knee level]." This runs counter to saying that there are no small jobs, just small people. Professor Whistler's former student did a poor job when unchallenged by the job that was too small, but rose to accomplish the most difficult, sometimes even impossible, tasks imaginable when properly challenged. Most of us are like this.

Dr. Charles Garfield, a psychologist with degrees in both psychology and mathematics, found this was particularly true of what he called "peak performance individuals." In working with NASA during the first launch of astronauts to the moon, Dr. Garfield was amazed to discover that many individuals who previously had done only mediocre work, and whom many considered "deadwood," had suddenly "caught fire" and were doing things neither they nor anyone else had even thought possible. Yet, immediately after the moon landings had been accomplished and the big challenge was over, it was like they "fell back to earth." Unchallenged, they returned to performing at their previous, only barely adequate levels. They and their superiors treated the whole peak performance and engagement experience as an aberration.[4] Too bad. Properly led, they could have continued to be challenged and to do the impossible far into the future. All it took was a little understanding and leadership. The leaders should have not only insisted on continual high standards for these others, but for themselves as well.[5]

Providing Workers with Information

Workers need high standards, but to reach these high standards they must be provided with all the information available on the matter. This is necessary whether the worker asks for this information or not. Although Drucker didn't go into this, if a worker isn't enthusiastic about acquiring information the leader feels is necessary to do the job, or doesn't know what information he needs, it is the manager's responsibility to explain the importance of that information and explain how to get it. Only with this kind of help can the worker control what he does, measure how he is doing, and guide himself toward reaching the goal and accepting complete responsibility for the task.

Moreover, it is critical the worker knows and understands how what he or she does contributes to the work of the entire organization and how the work of the organization contributes to society. This latter category of information is what many call "the big picture."[6] Information about the "big picture" helps employees acquire managerial vision, the last of the four paths Drucker identified for achieving employee engagement. Unfortunately, many managers attempt to lead by maintaining the ignorance of their subordinates. They keep control by showing their superior knowledge, withholding information or doling it out in small packages at strategic times to demonstrate their cleverness. Wrong, wrong, wrong!!! Do you want engaged members of your organization or do you want to be thought of as clever?

Encouraging Workers to Acquire Managerial Vision

Only with managerial vision can the worker feel the pride necessary for peak performance and see his work as contributing to the success of the enterprise. However, there are other important reasons why encouraging workers to gain managerial vision is necessary for peak performance and engagement. For example, the engaged worker must frequently operate without oversight, or even without the possibility of referral to higher authority when the boss is gone. Without managerial vision, the worker operating independently may optimize what he does at the expense of the organization. Moreover, operating at peak performance frequently requires taking risks. Yet a worker takes risks only with self-confidence. This means that worker self-confidence is also essential for engagement; self-confidence is gained through acquiring managerial vision.

* * *

Drucker taught us what we must do to attain high performance in our organizations—generate engaged workers—and he gave us the four actions we must take to accomplish this goal.

CHAPTER THREE

Drucker's Favorite Leadership Book

As I write these words, Doris Drucker, Peter Drucker's widow, is 101 years young.[1] She is bright, charming, and energetic. She exercises with weights, plays a mean game of tennis, and travels the world promoting Peter's values and ideas. Doris has accomplished much in her own right. She has a master's degree in physics from Fairleigh Dickinson University, an honorary doctorate from Claremont Graduate University, and became CEO of her own company, RSQ, an organization to manufacture and market a voice-volume monitor invented by herself and a partner in 1996. I consider her a good friend and she has been a wise mentor.

A couple years back, Doris Drucker was interviewed on video for a monthly video magazine then published by the Drucker School and was asked what management books Peter read. She divulged an important secret. Though he read business magazines and newspapers extensively, he only skimmed most management books. However, he did read many books on history, as he sought the lessons they offered that could be adapted to business management.

There was one leadership book, however, that Drucker not only read but also considered his favorite. He noted, "The first systematic book on leadership—the *Kyropaidaia* by Xenophon, himself no mean leader of men—is still the best book on the subject."[2] Despite all the books that have been published on leadership by well-known academic researchers and successful CEOs, he never altered that opinion. Xenophon's book, written around 400 B.C., was still the best, according to Drucker. "The scores of books, papers and speeches on leadership in business enterprise that come out every year have little to say on the subject that was not already old when the Prophets spoke and Aeschylus wrote."[3] Xenophon's advice was and is still applicable for today's executive.

Who Was Xenophon?

Who was this man whose writings on leadership the "Father of Modern Management" thought were the absolute best ever on the subject? Xenophon was a junior officer, part of a 10,000-man Greek army hired by the Persian pretender to the throne, Cyrus the Younger, to defeat his brother (King Artaxerxes II of Persia) in the fourth century B.C. At the time, the Greeks were considered the best infantrymen in the world. Cyrus thought that with these trained mercenary troops, he could defeat his brother's vastly superior force and seize the throne.

He was almost right. At first things went well and the Greek army appeared unbeatable. Unfortunately for the Greeks, in a crucial battle in Persia, Cyrus the Younger was killed. The victorious Persians invited the Greek generals to a feast, to be followed by negotiations to discuss the Greek army's withdrawal from Persia. All attendees on both sides were to be unarmed. You've heard the expression, "Beware of Greeks bearing gifts!"—that's a reference to the Trojan horse, but this was a Persian trap.

As soon as the unarmed Greek generals entered the Persian camp, they were cut off from any support and were massacred. The leaderless 10,000-man Greek army was now stranded thousands of miles from home and was surrounded by hostile forces. Undoubtedly this enhanced promotional opportunities in the Greek ranks. At a meeting to decide what to do, new leaders were elected and Xenophon was elevated to the rank of general. Apparently he had the articulation and charisma of a Barack Obama, as the young and relatively inexperienced Xenophon was soon made the general-in-chief.

In the book *The Persian Expedition*, Xenophon tells how he came to be overall commander and how he and his men fought to return to the Black Sea, battling against overwhelming odds every step of the way. This march to the sea, one of the most famous in ancient history, took five months. It is a story of courage, improvisation, and discipline, self-sacrifice, and, above all, leadership.

Inaction Is Worse Than No Action at All

After the Greek generals were killed, there was considerable fear in the Greek camp, but no one wanted to take action. Xenophon was not a general. He wasn't even a senior Greek officer. The 10,000 defeated men were just talking and voicing their fears. In their hearts, they knew that the Persians planned to attack them and sell them into slavery, but they were afraid to admit it, even to themselves. Many wanted to negotiate with the Persians. They thought they could reach some sort of arrangement to save their lives.

Think of British Prime Minister Neville Chamberlain and his negotiations with Adolf Hitler, during which he agreed to sacrifice the democratic state of Czechoslovakia in order to win a promise of peace. Chamberlain thought that this act would save lives and win "peace in our time." But Xenophon knew 2,000 years earlier that you can't do business with an aggressor. He asked himself, "What am I doing here doing nothing? What city is going to produce the general to take the right steps? Am I waiting to become a little older? If I don't take action, I'll never become older—I'll be dead!" So, Xenophon stepped forward and told his comrades that they had no hope in trying to negotiate. He explained what needed to be done. He spoke convincingly, and so they elected him as general and then overall commander.[4]

This is a lesson for all of us in business, no matter the size or nature of our organization. There is never a reason for inaction, whether or not there is an emergency. We must never take council of our fears, even when there is something to fear. There will always be those who say, "If we can just be understanding and give these fellows what they want, we can avoid fighting."

Xenophon knew that people must always face the facts and take whatever action needs to be taken, even if it is difficult and hazardous. As the saying goes, "Don't just stand there—do something!" And Xenophon did. He took charge and convinced his fellow Greeks not to surrender or to trust the Persians, who had already proven themselves untrustworthy by slaughtering their Greek leaders under a flag of truce.

Other Leadership Points from Xenophon

After becoming overall commander, and appointing his subordinate generals, Xenophon called them all together and gave them some important instruction in leadership:

1. You set the example. If you are downhearted, your men will become cowards. If you are clearly prepared to meet the enemy and call on your soldiers to do their part, you can be sure they will try to be like you.

2. You must hold yourself to be braver than the mass of men, and be the first to do the hard work.

3. You must be in control and exercise discipline, for when no one exercises control, nothing useful ever gets done.

4. You must get your soldiers thinking about what positive actions each must take to be successful; otherwise, they will think only about what is going to happen to them.[5]

When one soldier complained that he had to walk and carry a shield while Xenophon, who was wearing heavy cavalry armor, was mounted, Xenophon jumped from his horse, took the man's shield, and pushed him out of the ranks. Xenophon then led the pace and encouraged others, while carrying the shield and wearing the heavy cavalry breast plate as well. When the going was light, he led on horseback, but when the terrain was difficult or it was impossible to ride, he dismounted and led on foot.[6]

When some of his soldiers were disheartened because the Greeks had few cavalry, whereas the Persians had an abundance of mounted soldiers, Xenophon told them something that, centuries later, General George S. Patton would say to his army: "Wars may be fought with weapons, but they are won by men." But Xenophon put it this way: "Ten thousand cavalry only amount to ten thousand men. No one has ever died in battle by being bitten or kicked by a horse; it is men who do whatever gets done in battle."[7]

The same can be said about any human endeavor: It is men and women who get the job done and complete the project. So if your employees are despondent, or overly concerned about a lack of resources when compared with a competitor or in the situation they face, remember Xenophon: It is people, not horses, that win battles— or marketing campaigns, political campaigns, or anything else. This doesn't mean that resources count for nothing, but it does mean that they are not the deciding factor—people are. You can be successful with reduced resources, but not without committed people.

Servant Leadership Recommended by Xenophon 2,500 Years Ago

In 600 B.C., Cyrus the Great of Persia was a monarch who conquered the ancient Near East. Yet, according to Xenophon, Cyrus was a wise ruler who chose not to motivate his people by customary "carrot and stick." (We must remember that it was Xenophon writing this history. These events had occurred a couple hundred years earlier, so his account reflects some interpretation. Nevertheless, Xenophon was an experienced commander who recognized good decision making.) Here's Xenophon's story about Cyrus the Great when he was simply "Cyrus."

Cyrus's father once asked his son what he thought was the best way to motivate his followers. Cyrus answered: "After reflecting about these things, I think I see in all of them that which especially incites to obedience is the praising and honoring of one who obeys and the dishonoring of the one who disobeys."

Cyrus's father agreed that this was the way to gain obedience *by compulsion*, but he told his son that there was a far superior way in which human beings would obey "with great pleasure." Moreover he told him that when people think they will incur harm in obeying, they are not so ready to respond to the threat of punishments or to be seduced by gifts. However, this other method of attaining voluntary obedience worked even when there was danger. Cyrus continued, explaining that the method wasn't very complicated. He only had to look after his subordinates better than they would take care of themselves and ensure that he took care of them even before looking to his own interests.[8]

Who would not want to follow a leader who would look to others' interests before his own? Who would care more for individuals than himself? What do you think? Do you think that employees in your company might feel the same way and support a leader who thought more of them, as well as considered the organization's interests?

Some of Drucker's Thoughts on Xenophon

Of course, there is much more in Xenophon's writings about leadership, and many more valuable lessons for corporate leaders. Xenophon practiced leadership in a different time and a different place; his challenges were of a different type, yet the basic concepts hold true today. Drucker studied Xenophon's basis of leadership and combined it with his own experience, and the principles of integrity, commitment, and duty. These important lessons have in no way been improved upon by even the most recent research and writings on leadership. Whatever your leadership challenges, in whatever type of organization, you can learn much from Drucker's favorite book on leadership.

CHAPTER FOUR

The Seven Deadly Sins of Leadership

Peter Drucker set very high standards of ethics for leaders. He saw leaders as ordinary people who were "special" only because they had been entrusted with organizational and societal responsibilities. He knew that leaders were human and that they sometimes erred, and he was well aware that there were leaders who did not live up to the high standards he felt were not only necessary but also part of the code inherent in their acceptance of a position of leadership.

Some leaders fail to meet this obligation, whether to their profession, their organization, or the individuals they lead—or society itself. Some lose sight of the real goals they are expected to achieve and the reasons they became leaders in the first place. Others don't understand the implications of the responsibilities they have accepted, and they put their own interests above those they lead. Still others are seduced by the power and privileges that leadership brings. All of these failings pained Drucker, and he frequently wrote about them. His hope was that by exposing them, he could save leaders from falling into these traps.

The Seven Deadly Sins and Their Relation to Leadership

Peter Drucker didn't categorize as "sins" the character flaws that frequently cause leadership catastrophes. However, they recall the "seven deadly sins" about which the Roman Catholic Church has warned its followers since its earliest days. While Drucker's "sins" are not perfect matches for these, there are commonalities.

The Seven Deadly Sins is an ancient concept, mainly thought of today as a religious tenet originating in Christianity. Some say that they were based on an early interpretation of Israel's fight against the seven Canaanite tribes after fleeing Egypt. Others have found their origin in the book of Proverbs in the Old Testament, which lists the seven failings that God most abhors. What sins constitute the seven are not consistent; nevertheless, they point to important general beliefs. So it is easy to connect the old vices with the modern ones that Drucker cautioned against. Avoiding these "sins" might have saved many otherwise outstanding leaders or kept their organizations from disaster. In my opinion they are sins and they certainly can be deadly.

Is Pride Really So Bad?

The sin of pride is almost always considered the most serious, yet it seems so innocuous. My wife calls it "being full of oneself." Leaders feel proud of what they have accomplished or are accomplishing, and that is perfectly acceptable and justified. The problem comes in when leaders feel this pride to the extent that they believe themselves so special that ordinary rules no longer apply.

In Christian doctrine, pride caused the angel Lucifer to fall from Heaven and be transformed into Satan—pretty nasty consequences. Pride can also easily lead one to commit the other six sins. Sometimes even the perception of pride can have awful results.

Where Did All the Lust Come From?

I once heard a retired leader of a large organization speak about the challenges he faced while head of his organization. "One of the biggest problems," he said, "was newly promoted senior executives. I may be exaggerating a little, but it seemed almost as soon as we promoted a man to be a senior executive, he suddenly decided that he was God's gift to women."

This individual spoke of a time when almost all senior executives were male. However, the situation might be the same with female executives. Some leaders feel that they have "arrived" and are therefore entitled to sexual gratification as a fringe benefit of senior leadership. In an online survey done by the *White Stone Journal*, lust was the most frequent of sins self-reported, often termed "my biggest failing."[1] This sin is not uncommon. Moreover, it can have unfortunate consequences. In any workplace, sexual exploits create jealousies, feelings of favoritism, and a lack of trust. They damage people and relationships, and they also conflict with personal relationships outside of the organization.

As a basic human drive, sex is here to stay. However, when it is not confined to loving relationships outside of the office, there is trouble. We see newspaper stories about Roman Catholic cardinals being exposed for having covered up scandals of molestations by priests, followed by other stories reporting top Air Force generals testifying before Congress regarding extensive sexual misconduct by Air Force trainers at basic training in Texas. Who will quickly forget the foolish downfall of General David Petraeus, whom Secretary of Defense Robert Gates speculated history would regard as one of the United States' greatest battle captains?[2]

Avoiding this problem may mean rechanneling your sexual energy into other endeavors, or simply keeping your mind on your work; to do otherwise risks your good leadership position.

Greed Is NOT Good

The sin of greed is one of excess. Greed frequently starts with power. Leaders have power, and unfortunately having power tends to lead to being corrupt if the leader isn't careful. This situation may start with acceptance of small favors but it grows into vacations, loans, and worse.

Randy "Duke" Cunningham, a real hero during the Vietnam War, was wounded in action and received a Navy Cross, the highest award next to the Congressional Medal of Honor for bravery in battle. He was one of a handful of ace fighter pilots who shot down five or more enemy aircraft in that war. Cunningham remained in the Navy for twenty-one years. After leaving the Navy, he was elected to Congress and served for almost fifteen years. However, on November 28, 2005, he pled guilty to a variety of charges and resigned his seat in Congress. He admitted to taking $2.4 million in bribes from defense contractors and was sentenced to eight years, four months in prison.

This was the longest sentence ever given a former congressman in a corruption case. On receiving sentence, he said, "I misled my family, staff, friends, colleagues, the public—even myself. For all of this, I am deeply sorry. The truth is—I broke the law, concealed my conduct, and disgraced my high office."[3]

Laziness Is Unacceptable for the Leader

The sin of sloth causes an unwillingness to act. Sometimes this is due to laziness. More often it is a reluctance to take on work that the leader considers is now beneath him. I have seen leaders watching critical work that must be completed and that they were also qualified to do. Yet they stood around "supervising" when they could have pitched in and given real help.

In the last article that Drucker wrote for the *Wall Street Journal*, he stated that American CEOs were unique, having a position and set of responsibilities that did not exist in any other country. These responsibilities, Drucker said, included work that only the CEO could do but also that he must do.[4] In Drucker's view, these responsibilities involve connections outside the organization and decisions on what to do about them. Unfortunately, some CEOs abdicate these and many other responsibilities—failures that fall under the heading of sloth. Yes, all leaders, from whatever country, are always responsible, must be proactive, and must take action.

Anger Is the Enemy

The sin of wrath has to do with uncontrolled anger. There is a time for anger in leadership, when it serves a useful purpose. As Kenneth Blanchard and Spencer Johnson taught us in *The One-Minute Manager*,[5] you can take one minute to make a correction by including the words "I'm angry" and then tell the recipient why you are angry. Anger can mobilize another's psychological and physical resources to do something about a problem.

However, leaders need to avoid repeated and uncontrolled outbursts of anger because they will have major negative impact on leadership. Anger can destroy morale, while at the same time it does not guarantee a lasting result in correcting problems. Moreover, when someone is in an angry state, that anger causes the individual to lose the capacity for self-monitoring and the ability to observe objectively. In effect, the leader reserves the anger for times when expressing it can be both useful and appropriate.

Leaders Should Avoid Green Monsters

With the sin of envy, a leader allows his or her jealousy to override good judgment and integrity. Envy usually leads to decisions and actions that will put the object of that envy at a disadvantage. So a leader who falls victim to envy may deny an earned promotion to a qualified subordinate, attempt to destroy another's reputation, or in other ways try to make himself or herself feel better by lowering the reputation or situation of another. This is obviously harmful to the individual involved and to the organization. However, it is probably most harmful to the leader, who ultimately destroys his character and retards his ability to lead.

Good Leaders Seek Less Than Those Led

Most people associate food or drink with the sin of gluttony, but for the leader it has a far more ominous connotation. Of all the sins, gluttony was the one that most frustrated Drucker. Excessive consumption of any sort can be seen as a sign of status, and that's where the trouble begins.

Drucker defended perceived high executive salaries in his earlier writings. He knew how hard executives had to work to reach the pinnacle of their careers. However, skyrocketing executive salaries caused him to drastically alter his opinion. He said executive salaries at the top had clearly become excessive and that the ratios of compensation—top managers in relation to lowest paid workers—were the highest in the world. Moreover, this income difference wasn't slight—it differed by magnitudes. Drucker felt that this was morally wrong, and that we as a nation would end up paying a tremendous price for this. Indeed, in 2001, the ratio of average U.S. CEO compensation to average pay of a nonmanagement employee hit a high of 525 to 1.[6] At that point, Drucker recommended a ratio of no more than 20 to 1.[7]

Interestingly, Drucker drew a parallel between high executive salaries and the demands of unions for more and more benefits without increases in productivity. He predicted we would pay a terrible price for these examples of gluttony from both management and labor. "It is never pleasant to watch hogs gorge," he said. In fact, we have been paying this price for several years.

* * *

There are things that leaders must do, and things that they must not do. The seven deadly sins discussed here apply to leadership and are those things that Drucker maintained leaders must not do.

CHAPTER FIVE

Three Principles for Developing Yourself

Once a serious musician, Peter Drucker studied music composition under Austrian composer Anton Webern. Drucker knew he was progressing pretty well, but he got carried away with his success and wanted to compose what are known as "variations" at the same level as his instructor. His teacher chided him. "Peter, it took a genius like Joseph Haydn thirty years to attain the skill level to try what you propose. You will never be a Haydn, yet you want to do this though you have been at it less than thirty days."

After a year of work, Webern allowed Drucker to try a single, simple variation, cautioning him to be careful. Drucker proudly presented the product of his work. After examining the composition, Webern announced, "I was wrong . . . you aren't ready yet."

"He was right," remarked Drucker.[1] However, he was good enough, even after this failure, to continue toward becoming a professional musician. As we know, though, Drucker took another track. It, too, involved failure at first.

Principle One: Expect Some Failure, but Keep at It

Drucker accurately predicted many of the major developments that took place over the course of his lifetime. These included the rise of healthcare management, the future of online education for executives, Japan's rise as an economic world power, the decisive importance of marketing and innovation for any business, the emergence of the knowledge worker, the financial challenges resulting from a major recession, and much more. Yet Drucker failed in his first major public prediction. And, boy, was it a big mistake! Two weeks before "Black Tuesday," when the stock market plunged and the Great Depression began (October 29, 1929), Drucker wrote a newspaper column in which he predicted continual expansion of the stock market for the next decade.

Many Fail and Quit; A Few Try Again and Succeed

A would-be entrepreneur by the name of Rowland Macy tried valiantly to master the intricacies of founding and developing a retail store. He failed. He tried three more times, and each time he failed. It was not until his fifth attempt that he found success—great success. Today, Macy's and its affiliated stores have something like 180,000 employees and 800 stores in the United States alone.

Many others have experienced failures as they developed themselves into leaders:

- As a junior engineer at GE, Jack Welch, later named "Manager of the Century" by *Fortune* magazine, was almost fired. He had failed by mismanaging a project that blew the roof off a building.

- General Hoyt S. Vandenberg, the second Chief of Staff of the Air Force and one of its most outstanding World War II leaders, was almost dismissed from West Point for lack of leadership aptitude after his first year as a cadet.

- Warren Buffett is a wildly successful investor and industrialist who is consistently ranked as one of the wealthiest men in the world.

His first independent investment was a Sinclair Texaco gas station. It went bankrupt.

Our Two Greatest Presidents Had Initial Failures

Ask people who our two greatest presidents were, and they will probably name our first and sixteenth presidents: George Washington and Abraham Lincoln. Yet both were failures early on. George Washington began his military career as a young military officer by surrendering his first command during the French and Indian War. Twenty-five years later, he went on to win American independence as general-in-chief of the Continental Army, fighting for independence against the well-trained army of the major superpower of the day, Great Britain.

As a young man, Abraham Lincoln decided to get into politics. He ran for the Illinois General Assembly, with a number of advantages. He was a war hero, having served as a captain in the Blackhawk War; he was an amateur wrestler; and with an imposing stature of 6 feet 4 inches, it was said that he was tall and "strong enough to intimidate any rival." His townspeople liked and respected him. Also, Lincoln thought he had a good chance because, in the Illinois system, the top four people on the ballot were all sent to the assembly. Despite all of this, when the votes were counted Lincoln ranked eighth out of fifteen candidates. This didn't stop him from eventually being elected president, saving the Union, and abolishing slavery.

These are just a few examples that verify Principle One. A failure does not necessarily mean the end of the road if you are seeking to develop yourself into anything, and certainly it's not the end of the road if you intend to become a leader.

Principle Two: Volunteer, Make Mistakes, and Learn

Drucker had a strong belief about what could be learned from volunteering. He even recommended that all paid employees in corporations be treated as if they were unpaid volunteers, who could leave whenever they wished. Although this is less true during a recession, the *Los Angeles Times* reported recently that some employees were voluntarily leaving their jobs owing to dissatisfaction, despite an unemployment rate (in California) exceeding 10 percent at the time.

The fact that there are so many unpaid, volunteer jobs available means that anyone who wants one of these experiences can find one. These can be leadership positions in which to gain experience and develop yourself as a leader. And such opportunities exist not just in volunteer organizations but also in almost every company. I've told the following story many times. I do it because it is important—and true.

Example: The Power of Persuasion

There was a company that conducted savings bond drives every year. No one wanted the job of persuading other employees to sign up for additional deductions from their paychecks, even though the goal was to build savings. Most "volunteers" accepted the job only under pressure, and none did very well convincing others to make the investments. Yet as any successful manager will tell you, persuasion is an important part of achieving success; no one can become successful without the help of others.

One year, things changed dramatically in the engineering department. Somebody must have forgotten to tell the young engineer who volunteered, because he tried really hard to find investors. He was inexperienced as a leader and he made lots of mistakes, but he convinced many engineers and managers in his department to buy or increase their investments in savings bonds.

Because of the new volunteer's efforts, this department did better in the bond drive than any other department in the company. The president of the company took note and asked who had run the bond drive. He remembered this young engineer's name, and began a series of promotions that eventually resulted in the young engineer becoming a vice president.

Principle Three: Never Stop Learning

A proponent of lifelong education, Drucker never stopped learning. Continuous learning began as a concept in the German military in the early nineteenth century, when technology was advancing so rapidly that its strategy and tactics could no longer keep pace. A onetime mastery of the basics of the military profession was no longer acceptable, so the Germans institutionalized continuing, constant learning. From Europe, this concept spread to the U.S. military; in the early twentieth century, it began to be adopted by U.S. corporations as well. Some individuals saw it as a personal responsibility.

Drucker promoted lifelong learning for both individuals and organizations. He was an outstanding example, maintaining a program of reading and mastery of various subjects, following a highly organized method of development. His commitment to this self-development program is reflected in his ability to both write and speak with authority on a number of subjects and to apply this broad knowledge to whatever project he chose to focus on.

Example: Learning to Lead

It doesn't take much imagination to outline for yourself a development plan of leadership using this methodology of lifelong learning. For example, you can develop a reading list of books on leadership and apply the concepts laid out in each. I established such a list, read the books, and implemented just such a plan when I was barely a teenager. This helped me develop at a time when I had met failure earlier, owing to bad health.

Reoccurring rheumatic fever curtailed all athletic development for me for several critical years, beginning when I was seven. I say "critical" because, for young boys, athletic abilities are prime selectors, as well as advantages, for peer leadership positions. Suddenly thrust into the unwanted job of leading a Boy Scout patrol of a dozen other boys when I was thirteen, I lacked confidence and had no idea how to proceed. So, I was determined not to fail again as I had in the past. I found a book entitled *Handbook for Patrol Leaders*, published by the Boy Scouts of America. I read and followed its advice. To my surprise, although I had encountered setbacks, the advice worked. Not only was I able to lead, but my "Flaming Arrow" patrol soon excelled and won a number of awards. A year later, I was picked to be the Senior Patrol Leader, supervising three patrols. A year or so after that, I was made Junior Assistant Scoutmaster, the highest position a Boy Scout who was still a teenager could hold.

I learned Drucker's management principles from his writings and from being his student. But my own experience taught me that, no matter where you are in your personal development, the learning never ends.

* * *

For success, follow these three Drucker principles:

1. Expect some failure, but keep at it.

2. Volunteer, make mistakes, and learn.

3. Never stop learning.

CHAPTER SIX

Move Your Company Ahead by Encouraging Your People

To Peter Drucker, management was more than a job, even more than a profession. It was a calling. So, managers were certainly not supposed to cause harm. This doesn't mean that managers should not strive for efficiency in what they or others do, or that they aren't responsible for performance in their areas of work. Rather, it is that being the boss is not like a switch that you turn on and forget. Leading others consists of always respecting and helping those you lead and work with, not driving them hard while you focus on competing with others for your own success.

Max DePree is the former chairman and CEO of Herman Miller, Inc., the furniture maker that *Fortune* magazine once named one of the ten "best managed" and "most innovative" companies in America. DePree wrote: "The best people working for organizations are like volunteers. Since they could probably find good jobs in any number of groups, they choose to work somewhere for reasons less tangible than salary or position. Volunteers do not need contracts, they need covenants."[1]

Peter Drucker taught the same thing. In the modern world, where employees have mobility, even in a recession, all employees should be treated as if they were volunteers and can go somewhere else—because they can. And "volunteer treatment" is a strong form of giving employees the most help.

Treating People with Respect Gains Respect

Isn't it within your power as a manager to treat people with respect and to ensure that others in your organization do the same? Certainly every human being deserves to be treated with respect. Many outstanding leaders maintain that those who work for you should be treated with even more than respect. Mary Kay Ash, the woman who built a billion-dollar corporation, Mary Kay Cosmetics, recommended that managers imagine that everyone they meet every day is wearing a large sign saying, MAKE ME FEEL IMPORTANT.

James MacGregor Burns, an American political scientist, wrote an excellent book called *Leadership*. (In fact, the book was so outstanding that it won the Pulitzer Prize.) Here's his succinct advice, for Drucker could not have put it much better himself: "In real life, the most practical advice for leaders is not to treat pawns like pawns, nor princes like princes, but all persons like persons."[2] Drucker followed this advice. He treated virtually everyone with respect. I suspect that not only CEOs, but also heads of state were treated exactly the way he treated his students.

Recognition for Good Work Is Desired and Deserved

Everyone wants recognition, according to Connie Podesta and Jean Gatz, two management consultants who wrote *How to Be the Person Successful Companies Fight to Keep*. They reported that one CEO confided his frustration and distress:

> I have worked so hard to turn this company around. I have managed to keep our profits up without laying off one person. I provide excellent benefits, and I'm willing to pay for my employees to go to

school. I spend a great deal of money on picnics, parties, and celebrations because I want them to enjoy their jobs and feel as though this is a family they can count on. Very few of them have ever said thank you or even seem to appreciate how hard I try to make this a great place to work. On the other hand, if one little thing goes wrong or I have to say no to any of their ideas, some of them threaten to quit. And others won't speak to me.[3]

You may feel that this is the nature of workers and that this CEO must learn to be more thick-skinned. Perhaps. But here is an important manager, a CEO who has made it to the top of his company. He has power and responsibility, and is probably making a good salary. Yet even he craves recognition for what he does for his workers. If this is true of a powerful person like this, think how true it must be for everyone else—including you and me, and those you may wish to motivate.

There are so many ways to recognize your employees. Management expert Dr. Bob Nelson, a friend who completed the same doctoral program under Drucker that I did, actually identified over a thousand! He published them in a book entitled *1001 Ways to Reward Employees*. If you think that's a lot (and it is!), Bob recently updated his book with a new one: *1501 Ways to Reward Employees*.[4]

Workers Need to Develop Their Skills

Do you create opportunities for those in your organization to develop their skills? Can you provide special courses in-house? How about a few hours off every week to complete a college degree? Maybe you can hire a physical fitness instructor to work with employees during lunch or after work. Sometimes an employee has the ability to do this, or has unique knowledge about which he or she is willing to instruct other employees. All you need to do is ask. Don't forget that you and other managers or workers in your organization can act as teachers if any of you have expertise in special areas. Of course, those who teach also learn.

Let Your Workers Think for Themselves

Are you open to letting your people think for themselves? Drucker said that you *could* tell people what to do; however, he also taught that managers must allow their workers to decide how to do most parts of their jobs for themselves—that it motivated workers to do so. Peter Drucker didn't mean that you shouldn't give help if asked. However, you need to recognize that people have their own abilities, experiences, and unique backgrounds. That's why they have been given the duties that they have been assigned. That's also why they're such valuable resources: They have a lot to contribute. It's wasteful to do all of the thinking for everyone in your organization. Try that, and sooner or later you are certain to run into difficulties.

Even if you could do all of the thinking for all of your workers, you would be ill-advised to do so. If all of your people thought exactly like you, your organization would have a pretty limited source of ideas. In addition, researchers have discovered that synergy is created such that the products of many separate brains working together are far greater than the sum of each considered separately. If you try to do all the thinking in your organization yourself, you will lose this important synergism. Let your workers do their own thinking, and you'll be amazed and surprised at what they come up with and how they use their expertise to solve your problems.

A business scientist by the name of Frederick Herzberg built on Maslow's work involving motivation and needs. Herzberg collected data on job attitudes among employees in hundreds of companies. From studying the data, he concluded that workers have two completely different categories of needs that affect satisfaction or dissatisfaction with a job.

According to Herzberg, real motivators are satisfying factors that relate to the job itself. They involve feelings of achievement, recognition for accomplishment, challenging work, increased responsibility, growth, and development. These are the factors that produce job satisfaction as contrasted with the other category, "hygiene needs," which only prevent job dissatisfaction.

Herzberg's work is important to us because it means that if we reduce the hygiene factors, we're going to get job dissatisfaction. How would you feel if someone reduced your salary? So to avoid job dissatisfaction, we maintain the hygiene factors at their present levels. Of course, there are exceptions to this rule. Most workers will accept reduction for the good of the organization if everyone's salary is reduced proportionately on a fair basis.

However, if we want those we lead to be more satisfied with their jobs, we must use the real motivators, not only salary. That is, we must look for ways that we can increase:

- Feelings of achievement

- Recognition

- Challenge in the work

- Responsibility

- Growth and development

What Does It Cost to Give Workers What They Really Want?

Most of the factors considered important by workers can probably be improved by you today. These are factors that you can improve regardless of restrictions or limitations on salary or benefits placed by your parent organization. And none of these will cost you very much to implement compared with pay, benefits, or providing perfect job security. This is good news if you have limited resources and want to motivate and help your workers achieve higher performance.

While you are helping others in your company, you will help your company get ahead at the same time. That's the Peter Drucker way to success for your organization: Care for your people, and it will be a win-win for you and them, and a win for your organization. He meant what he said in teaching us that, above all, do no harm. He wanted us to succeed with our organizations, and he knew that the way to do this was a focus not only on goals but on people as well.

CHAPTER SEVEN

The Most Important Leadership Decision

Peter Drucker, the "Father of Modern Management," taught us that the first and most important leadership decision to be made is the decision to become a leader. Like much of Drucker's advice, this pronouncement sounds self-evident, overly simplified, and even a trifle absurd. The truth is that it is profoundly true and important. For someone who has never been a leader previously, acceptance of the responsibilities of a leader is frequently not an easy decision to make.

Many who have never had the responsibility and authority of leadership fear both. They fear something going wrong, they fear being blamed for actions that they do not think will be fully under their control, they fear that followers will not follow, and they fear making the wrong decision. Many would-be leaders are afraid of the embarrassment and penalties of failure. Some individuals who have the capability of becoming great leaders never accept the challenge. They go through life with a fear that limits the success they could achieve and the contributions they might make by helping others.

Whether you are an executive, and it is your job to develop knowledge workers and to help nonleaders make this decision, or you are a professional trying to make your own decision about whether to become a leader, please read on. Drucker's wisdom can help you and have a major impact on your life.

No One Is Born to Leadership

Everybody starts equally as would-be leaders and faces these fears of the responsibility, authority, and the unknown of leadership, and this is true regardless of age. Mary Kay Ash built the billion-dollar Mary Kay Cosmetics Corporation by beginning with only $5,000. When she was just three years old, her father was invalided with tuberculosis and couldn't take care of himself. Her mother went to work to support the family. Mary Kay accepted the duties of cleaning, cooking, and caring for her father. She accepted the responsibility; she had the authority for domestic decisions and ran the household during the day.

Mary Kay made the Drucker decision to be a leader when she was still a child and before she even knew what leadership was. The lessons she learned early on helped her to reach her full potential later. As is frequently the case, what appears to be an unfair challenge, suddenly being given the responsibility for caring for a father, mother, sister, brother, grandparent, or other relative, forces people to learn leadership, like it or not. Even the tragedy of being forced to care for a drunken parent as a teenager has frequently resulted in someone's appearing to be a "natural leader" somewhat later in life.

Corporal York Is Forced to Be a Leader

Alvin C. York was raised in the backwoods of Tennessee, where he became an expert rifleman. Until he met his future wife and became religious, he was a heavy drinker and troublemaker. No one noticed anything particularly unusual about him when he was drafted into the Army for service during World War I. That is, until he filed to avoid military service as a conscientious objector. His company commander convinced him that his country needed him and he should remain in the army. York withdrew his request to avoid service and went overseas to France with his unit. The needs of his fellow soldiers forced him into a leadership role. His success as an unofficial leader was recognized and he was promoted to the rank of corporal.

On October 18, 1918, York was sent on a patrol in the Argonne Forest with sixteen other men under the command of a sergeant. The patrol managed to surprise a German headquarters and took several prisoners. As the patrol moved on, they stumbled on a hidden nest of enemy machine guns that opened fire with deadly effectiveness. Only York and seven privates survived the first volley of enemy fire. They now faced an entire machine-gun battalion consisting of several hundred enemy soldiers. York had almost no leadership training. He was a young corporal with seven other soldiers in a very perilous situation.

Those with York talked about surrender, but they agreed to follow a plan he suggested. They would remain concealed and would fire only when they would not be revealing their position. York would use the skills he had learned in the Tennessee woods and his expertise as a marksman to keep the enemy battalion at bay until night came and they could escape. So skillfully did York attack the enemy, and so accurate was his rifle fire, that his foes suffered numerous casualties as York maneuvered around the area, rarely even seen by his adversaries. At one point, an entire enemy squad of a dozen infantrymen attacked his position. He shot every single one. The enemy commander became convinced that he was under attack by a far superior force that he could not see. He was suffering many casualties and could do nothing to defend himself. Finally, he raised the white flag and surrendered. Before the end of the day, York and his seven-man patrol had captured 132 prisoners, including three officers.

The Supreme Allied Commander, French Marshal Ferdinand Foch, had been at war for four years. He was aware of the daily actions of millions of men in battle. He saw hundreds of situations where courageous leaders performed heroic deeds under fire. Yet, Foch called York's feat the greatest individual action of the war. General John J. Pershing, the overall American commander, immediately promoted York to sergeant and recommended him for the Congressional Medal of Honor—America's highest decoration for valor. Sergeant York received his medal shortly thereafter.

After the war, York returned to Tennessee. He married his girlfriend and became a farmer. He turned down all offers to use his name for profit, saying, "This uniform isn't for sale." However, he did allow a movie of his life to be made, and he used the proceeds to establish schools for poor mountain children. *Sergeant York* won two Oscars, one for Gary Cooper as Best Actor and one for Best Editing, and it was nominated in nine other categories, including Best Picture. During World War II, York, as a colonel, commanded a regiment of the Tennessee National Guard.

Some Don't Know They're Ready for Leadership

Sudden leadership responsibilities don't only occur in battle. Jonathan Avery was a forty-five-year-old human resources manager who worked for an aerospace company. Jonathan knew his stuff. Many times he had been asked whether he was interested in management responsibilities. However, like so many others, he had never in his life been in a position of leadership and he was doing well as a human resources specialist, so he declined. However, one day things got desperate when a much younger team leader became seriously ill and had to go on an extended leave of absence. With promises from his boss of help if needed, he agreed to being acting department manager.

The fact that he was such a good human resources specialist enabled Jonathan to provide better than average help and guidance to his team. With the help of his boss, he mastered the challenge and by the time the permanent manager returned, Jonathan was immediately promoted to a position with permanent leadership responsibilities. "If I hadn't been forced by the situation, and persuaded by my manager,

I would never have even tried such a thing," he told me. As so many others who have been thrust into leadership have found out, being a leader is definitely doable once you get into it and do your best.

A Boy's Story

Some years ago, a thirteen-year-old boy had joined the Boy Scouts. He had always been an introvert and very shy. Moreover, an early childhood disease had left him thin and weak. He had never been a leader. His scout troop announced a contest to see who could master the most scouting skills during a six-month period. The boy applied himself and won the contest.

Then the boy's father was transferred to Texas. In this new town, the one troop where it seemed most likely he would fit in hadn't been doing very well. However, the troop had a new Scoutmaster and he had plans to rebuild the troop. This Scout troop had two patrols with about a dozen members in each, but one had recently lost its patrol leader. The Scoutmaster told this boy that he wanted him to be patrol leader because of the scouting skills he had mastered. The boy had all the normal fears about leadership described earlier, so he declined. Only when the Scoutmaster promised to help him if he ran into problems did he accept and make the decision that Drucker said is the most important.

The boy worked hard and found that he liked being a leader. Moreover, in every competition between the two patrols, his patrol was judged best. In a statewide competition, with many patrols, his patrol again won awards. A year later, the Scoutmaster appointed him senior patrol leader, responsible for both patrols. I know about this boy intimately, because it was me. While I refined my leadership skills later—in high school, at West Point, in the Air Force, and in civilian organizations that I led—without that Scoutmaster's help in persuading me to make "Drucker's decision on leadership," as I reported in Chapter 5, my life would have taken an entirely different course.

* * *

If you have a subordinate who hasn't yet made this most important of leadership decisions, you can help him or her to do so by:

- Assigning small, short-term leadership tasks in order to build self-confidence

- Providing assistance and mentorship as the new leader develops, typically by making mistakes

- Giving encouragement and inspiration

If you are yourself someone who has not yet made Drucker's leadership decision, I recommend you take the plunge. Just making the decision that you will be a leader will help you to become one.

CHAPTER EIGHT

Drucker and Heroic Leadership

In 1978, the Pulitzer Prize–winning author James MacGregor Burns published his now classic book *Leadership*. In it he placed leadership into two categories: transactional and transformational. *Transformational* leadership was the preferred process, in that it was more potent and engaged the full person of the follower. Leaders and followers stimulated each other to advance followers into leaders and might even convert leaders into moral agents. The transformational approach clearly has much to recommend it, including significant positive change in people and organizations, changes in perceptions and values, and changes in the expectations and aspirations of those led. In short, transformational leaders are idealized because they are not focused on benefits to themselves, but on benefits for the organization, its members, and those they serve.

According to Burns, *transactional* leadership is based on the exchange relationship of simple reward for obedience or punishment for disobedience. Many have criticized heroic leadership on this basis. There is even a "postheroic-leadership" type recommended by some leadership experts today in which organizations supposedly operate, or should operate, that espouses a lack of hierarchical control where members essentially lead the organization themselves and the leader is mostly a figurehead and cheerleader. How did Drucker see it?

The Origin of Heroic Leadership

To fully understand Drucker's views, we need to look at the origins of what today is called "heroic leadership." Interestingly, it was the same Burns who introduced the concept. But it wasn't as some think. Perhaps misled by a misunderstanding of what the name represented, some have corrupted Burns's concept of heroic leadership, such that it has become the ultimate representative of the less desirable transactional type and of much that has gone wrong within organizations in recent years. Yet Burns introduced heroic leadership not as an example of transactional leadership but clearly as an example of the preferred transformational type.[1,2]

Drucker's Complaint

Drucker did not agree with the interpretations of heroic or postheroic leadership. For example, he wrote and taught that there is no such thing as successful laissez-faire leadership, and that there must always be a leader responsible for directing an organization. That is, someone has to be in control. Even participative leadership was not a universal cure.

Referring to Douglas McGregor's Theory X and Theory Y, Drucker maintained that while the participation of members in decision making was desirable in many instances, there were times when Theory X (a directive style) was more effective than Theory Y (a participative style). Limited time for action might be one example. He pointed out that McGregor himself had written that he had never intended to recommend one theory over the other, only that management should analyze and determine in which situations each theory might be best applied.[3,4]

Things Go Awry with Laissez-Faire Leadership

Drucker wrote that his friend and leadership expert, Warren Bennis, had tried implementing Theory Y in a more or less laissez-faire fashion in an attempt to raise achievement at the University of Buffalo during Bennis's tenure as president of that institution. As Drucker relates, "There was tremendous excitement but also total failure. Instead of achievement, there was lack of direction, lack of objectives, lack of controls, and frustration." While pointing out that simply adopting Theory Y was not what was intended by McGregor, Drucker also stated that by itself Theory Y was inadequate and was not necessarily a new, better, or morally superior way of leading.

Lessons from the Ancients

Drucker further showed that the concepts of transformational leadership were known and practiced by the ancients several thousands of years ago. They confirmed Burns's concept regarding the categorization of heroic leadership as a transformational type. Drucker looked to historical documents for confirmation.

One example was Drucker's favorite leadership book, *Kyropaidaia*, which is sometimes translated as *The Education of Cyrus the Great*. As we discussed in Chapter 3, Drucker described it as the first systematic book on leadership, and still the best. The book was written by Xenophon, a Grecian general turned historian and author, about 2,005 years ago.[5] It is full of examples of how to lead, using the metaphor of Cyrus the Great of Persia's learning and practicing leadership some 200 years before Xenophon's writings.

Xenophon wrote that Cyrus chose not to motivate primarily by the "carrot or stick" method—that is, the exchange method that defines transactional leadership. Cyrus's father convinced his son that, while he could gain obedience by compulsion, it was better to try a different approach: take care of his subordinates better than they would take care of themselves and take care of them even before his own welfare. Not only was this a superior way to gain obedience from his people, but they would do so "with great pleasure."

Notice that there are no exchange concepts here. Xenophon suggested other aspects of good leadership that are suspiciously like transformational types currently recommended by most leadership experts today.

The Importance of Control

Xenophon also recommended to his readers: "Be in control and exercise discipline, for when no one exercises control, nothing useful ever gets done." Detractors of heroic leadership sometimes use the term "command and control" in referencing the type of leadership that should be avoided. Yet both Xenophon and Drucker maintained that control is a necessity for good leadership.

The term "command and control" is a military one. Its official definition is "the exercise of authority and direction by a properly designated commander over assigned and attached forces in the accomplishment of a mission."[6] It refers to a military commander's authority to have his legal orders obeyed. The term does not refer to leadership. It is simply a source of power, as are position, expertise, likability, and the like. Organizational leaders in civilian life have similar authority. However, among nonmilitary people, the term "command and control" leadership has come to mean a leader who leads through simply giving orders and demanding obedience. By this definition, "command and control" refers to a leader who uses a single behavioral influence strategy, direction, and has an authoritative, as opposed to a participative, style.

According to proponents, the so-called postheroic leader operates in a role in which there is little direct control. Instead, the postheroic leader leads only through influence. This is a simple, but gross misunderstanding of heroic leadership. The heroic leader always leads through influence, whether that influence is direct or indirect. Direction is necessary, for example, when time is a major factor or direction may be the only effective influence behavioral strategy that is likely to work. Yet a heroic leader may also use indirection by issuing no direct orders at all in leading. Both of these are part of his or her repertoire as a leader to be called on as appropriate to the situation.

Using Indirection to Save a Life

I heard a story once about a woman who was poised on the suspension of a bridge, determined to commit suicide by jumping into the waters far below. A policeman called to the woman to persuade her to climb back to safety. He tried logic and failed. He tried to order her down. That didn't work, either. All attempts failed and spectators realized that the woman was determined to jump. Finally, the policeman called to her and said: "Lady, you can jump if you want, but I sure wouldn't want to jump into that dirty water. It's full of sewage and garbage, and smells awful." The woman hesitated, and then climbed back to the safe part of the bridge. Eventually others were able to get her to safety.

* * *

Drucker did not use the term "heroic leadership." Yet his numerous writings and speeches made it clear that the right kind of leader was someone special, someone who would put subordinates, customers, and mission before himself to ensure that in leading, the leader would be fulfilling Drucker's own definition of leadership: "the lifting of a man's vision to higher sights, the raising of a man's performance to a higher standard, the building of a man's personality beyond its normal limitations." That's heroic leadership in a nutshell.

CHAPTER NINE

What Everyone Knows
Is Usually Wrong

He's rarely quoted on this, but it was one of Peter Drucker's most common cautions to us in his classroom and it was an expression he often used outside of class. "What everyone knows is usually wrong," he claimed. This sounds so wrong in itself that I was certain when I first wrote about this Druckerism that he must have actually said *frequently* wrong, not *usually* wrong. However, recently some old classroom notes have come to light and there's no mistake. What Drucker said was, "What everyone knows is *usually* wrong." Now, it is true that Drucker many times uttered statements to make a particular point. This made him, as one friend stated, "eminently quotable." But could Drucker have absolutely meant what he said in this case? I eventually concluded that, crazy as it sounds, he *did* mean it, and moreover that he was right.

I need to explain. I'm not talking about scientific facts, like the law of gravity or $E = mc^2$, and neither was Drucker. He was talking about opinion expressed as fact. After much thought, I concluded that this seemingly simple and self-contradicting statement is amazingly true; and not only that, once accepted and applied, it is immensely valuable—and not only in business.

What Drucker wanted to emphasize was that we must always question our assumptions, no matter from where they originate. This is especially so regarding anything that a majority of people "know" or assume without questioning. This "knowledge" should always be suspect and needs to be examined much closer because, in a surprisingly high percentage of cases, the information "known to be true" will turn out to be inaccurate or completely false. This can lead to extremely poor, even disastrous management decisions. It also leads to an incredible number of stupid laws pandering to prejudices and propaganda that are repeated, through ignorance or malice, in direct contradiction to facts, which many times are readily available and easily uncovered.

Things Once "Known to Be True" Are Now Known to Be False

Of course, there are many old "truisms" once thought by everyone to be true that we laugh at today. "The world is flat" or "The earth is the center of the universe" is typical. The ancient Greeks "knew" that everything was made up of only four elements: earth, air, fire, and water. Of course, in modern times we have learned that they were mistaken. When I took chemistry in high school, I learned that a periodic table of elements had been formulated by a fellow named Mendeleev, and that it had been established that there were exactly ninety-three elements—no more, no less. We got an "A" if we could name them all; I'm sure we would have been given an "F" if we intimated that there were more than 93 elements. Today, though, there are 118 elements—or so "everybody knows."

Many Things "Known" Today Are Just Plain Wrong

Just about everyone, both Christian and non-Christian alike, knows that the Immaculate Conception refers to the birth of Jesus, right?

Maybe so, but what everybody knows is wrong again. According to the *Catholic Encyclopedia*, the Immaculate Conception refers to the fact that "Mary was preserved exempt from all stain of original sin at the first moment of her animation, and sanctifying grace was given to her before sin could have taken effect in her soul."[1]

Or consider the most famous sentence uttered by Sir Arthur Conan Doyle's famous detective, Sherlock Holmes. Out of Conan Doyle's four published novels and fifty-six short stories about the adventures of Sherlock Holmes and his sidekick and physician friend, Dr. John H. Watson, everyone knows that this famous sentence consisted of only the four words: "Elementary, my dear Watson."

According to what everyone knows, Holmes would respond with these words on Dr. Watson's surprise at a particularly shrewd deduction made by the sleuth. Sorry. What everyone knows is wrong again. Holmes never said these immortal words in a single instance in four novels and fifty-six short stories written by Conan Doyle. If not from Conan Doyle's literary character, where did these words come from? They came out of the mouth of the English actor Basil Rathbone. He played the part of Sherlock Holmes in a popular series of Hollywood movies in the 1930s and 1940s, which were based on Conan Doyle's famous detective. It was Rathbone who uttered the famous response that came to represent Holmes's character. I hasten to add that these words seemed to fit Conan Doyle's hero so well that maybe Holmes should have said them in print. But alas, he did not.

The Collective Wisdom of the Sanhedrin

Interestingly, Drucker's lesson goes beyond the millennia. In ancient Israel, the highest court was called the Sanhedrin. It corresponded roughly to the U.S. Supreme Court, although it had a lot more power. The Sanhedrin tried the most important cases, and it had the power to exact capital punishment. In this high court, there were no prosecuting or defense attorneys and no appeals. The Sanhedrin court consisted only of top judges. Some historians say there were seventy-one judges, others say twenty-three. The actual number is unimportant to some factual points.

The judges could examine the defendant, the accusers, and any witnesses either side brought before it. To exonerate a defendant required a majority of one, while to find him guilty required a majority of two. But perhaps the most interesting aspect of this ancient Jewish legal body was that if all judges found the accused guilty of a capital crime, he or she was allowed to go free! This was because the ancient Hebrews were convinced that there is a defense to be argued for every individual accused, regardless of the gravity of the crime and the persuasiveness of the evidence. If not a single learned judge considered that the defendant's case had at least enough merit to raise doubt, then it was clear evidence to them that, no matter how definite the circumstances, something was wrong in the situation and it was possible that the accused was innocent. In other words, when every judge knew something to be true, it probably wasn't.

In modern times, the impact of mass agreement on an issue has been addressed and confirmed in psychological research. In one experiment, subjects were to rate the attractiveness of individuals depicted in selections of photographs. However, there was only one real subject and the results were rigged. Unknown to this one subject, the other participants were part of the scientist's team of experimenters. These participants always agreed about the most attractive individual depicted in any particular set of photographs, even if their choice was definitely not the most attractive. It was found that the subject could usually be influenced to agree with any photograph that the group selected, regardless of merit. This experiment demonstrates the influence of social proof while it confirms one reason why Drucker's assertion that what everyone knows is usually wrong is correct.

Drucker's Wisdom Is Critical in Business

Is Drucker's wisdom on common "knowledge" valid or important in business? In 1982, someone laced a popular over-the-counter drug with cyanide. Several who bought the poisoned product died. This led to an almost instantaneous nationwide panic. One hospital received 700 queries from people suspecting they had been poisoned with the tainted product. People in cities across the country were admitted to hospitals on suspicion of cyanide poisoning. The Food and Drug Administration (FDA) investigated 270 incidents of suspected product tampering. While some of the product had been tampered with as some sort of a sick joke, in most cases this was pure hysteria, with no basis at all in fact. This panic in itself demonstrates part of Peter Drucker's thesis, but there is more that is of some importance to business decision makers.

At that time, the product had been established for almost thirty years. Over the years, it had built up a well-deserved trust with consumers. Nevertheless, sales of the product plummeted overnight and Johnson & Johnson, the product's maker, launched a recall and stopped all sales. The company advised its own customers not to buy or use the product until further notice.

Virtually everyone predicted the demise of the product. One well-known advertising guru was quoted in the *New York Times:* "I don't think they can ever sell another product under that name. . . . There may be an advertising person who thinks he can solve this and if they find him, I want to hire him, because then I want him to turn our water cooler into a wine cooler."[2]

The product once dominated the market. "Everyone knew" that those days were gone for good. An article in the *Wall Street Journal* commented sadly, as if in an obituary, that the product was dead and could not be resurrected; any other notion was an executive's pipe dream. A survey of "the man in the street" found almost no one who would buy the product regardless of what the company did to guarantee its safety or promote its sale.

Despite "what everyone knew," Johnson & Johnson retained the product Tylenol and its now famous brand name, which had become infamous through no fault of the product or its maker. Johnson & Johnson launched one of the most effective public relations campaigns for a product in commercial history. As a result, sales began a steady climb only a few months after the poisonings. Tylenol rose to once again become the number one analgesic, and controls about 35 percent of a $2 billion market.

Where would Johnson & Johnson be today had this established brand, built through thirty years of advertising, performance, and reliability, been allowed to disappear? How much would it have cost Johnson & Johnson to attempt to introduce and build an entirely new brand to replace Tylenol? Could this have even been accomplished? We'll never know. Nor do we know whether Peter Drucker was called in to consult with Johnson & Johnson.

What we do know is that Johnson & Johnson did the right thing when this tragedy struck and then took the right actions to reintroduce the Tylenol product successfully despite "what everybody knew." These actions today are studied in the business schools as an almost perfect example of a successful public relations strategy and execution, as well as being the right thing to do ethically. However, the basis of this conclusion was that Johnson & Johnson executives, knowingly or not, decided, "What everyone knows is usually wrong." They ignored what all the experts—and even the consumers—"knew" and went on to resurrect Tylenol to be even more successful than it was previously.

* * *

Drucker's lesson? Before you take advice or recommendations, even from those who should know, don't forget that what everybody knows is usually wrong. Refuse to accept "common knowledge" or "what everybody knows" without careful examination.

CHAPTER TEN

Power Comes from Integrity

Peter Drucker is known as the "Father of Modern Management" because his concepts revolutionized the way we manage. In discussing integrity, he showed that it can mean a lot of different things to different people, but he simplified it to a single sentence: "Integrity means adhering to a code of ethics and doing the right thing by sticking to that code." He was very clear that personal integrity was a part of business integrity, and doing the right thing in business and professional life was immensely powerful for both the individual and the corporation. People frequently cannot believe that simple integrity can be so effective or can have such a significant positive impact. Well, it absolutely can. And here's proof.

The Power of Integrity

Hamlin "Ham" Tallent was a Naval Flight Officer, or NFO. As an F-14 squadron commander on an aircraft carrier, Ham's squadron and another squadron were in competition for a Battle "E" award, and one of the primary criteria was the number of hours flown by squadron members. Turns out they should have won, but the other squadron was fudging the number of hours logged. Since the competition was cheating, Ham's pilots wanted to do the same. He absolutely refused. So honesty won out, and Ham's squadron got the Battle "E" award, right? Wrong. The cheaters got the award. But that wasn't the end of the story.

Over the next twenty years or so, almost every pilot in the squadron that cheated left the Navy, for one reason or another. But almost every pilot in Ham's squadron not only stayed in the Navy but also contributed significantly to our country's defense. As a group, they tended to have unusually successful careers. The documenter of this true story, a former Navy Seal, now a business leader, wrote: "Good leaders beget good leaders, and under Ham's influence a large number of Navy leaders of whom the nation can be proud were groomed." And Hamlin Tallent himself? He went on to become a rear admiral, a senior leader in the Navy despite the fact that his squadron didn't win the Battle "E" award when he was on the way up.[1]

My Own Story of the Power of Personal Integrity

Believe it or not, I can tell a very similar story. The Air Force version of the Navy's NFO was called a "navigator." I was one. I first wrote about this incident in a book of mine on leadership. Some of the individuals I had interviewed for the book preferred to remain anonymous. I decided to do the same in this instance and identified the protagonist not as myself, but as "Herb." However, in a speech sometime after publication, I told the story in the first person. Someone in the audience who had read my book thought that I had stolen "Herb's" story—pretty ironical for a story that was supposed to be an example of personal integrity. Since then, I've explained that I was "Herb." Anyway, here is "Herb's" story and how it affected my future in a way I never expected.

As a newly minted lieutenant, Herb was the new navigator on a B-52 nuclear bomber. Among Herb's responsibilities was the programming and launch of the two air-to-ground "cruise" missiles called "Hound Dogs." The missiles were new and there were still many problems with them. Those in Herb's squadron who had flown with them got mixed results. Sometimes the missiles were right on target. More often, they went far from where intended.

The aircrew didn't really launch the missiles. That would have been much too expensive, as each missile cost millions of dollars. The navigator programmed them in the air, constantly updating their information. This took several hours. About thirty minutes from the target, he put the missiles into a "simulated launch" mode and then instructed the pilots to follow a compass-like needle indicator on their consoles. If the needle turned right, the pilots turned the aircraft right. If the needle turned left, they turned the aircraft left. When they did this, the aircraft followed the course to the target according to information in the missile's computer and inertial guidance system.

Fifteen seconds from the target, Herb turned on a tone signal that was broadcast over the radio. On the ground, a Ground Control Intercept (GCI) site tracked Herb's aircraft on radar. At the point where the missile would normally dive into its target, the missile would automatically terminate the tone signal. The course the missile would take to the ground once it started its final dive was based on predetermined factors. Using this information, the GCI site calculated where the missile would have impacted if it had actually been launched.

These practice impacts had a major effect on the crews' careers. Those who got good scores got promoted. Those who did not were held back. Herb's five crewmates were all far more experienced than he was. They were senior in rank and were combat veterans of both World War II and Korea. Herb was fresh out of flying school. He had never been in combat and had never even served on an aircrew before.

All aircrews were having problems with these new missiles. However, it hadn't mattered yet because all were given six months to learn to work with the missiles without penalty, so the bad scores didn't count. What no one knew at the time was that it was not the aircrews causing the problems, but the extreme sensitivity of the missiles and the more complex techniques required by those who maintained and serviced the missiles' computer and navigation guidance systems on the ground. However, the six-month period of learning had expired. While on seven-day alert, Herb's aircraft commander called the crew together. "When we fly our first training mission after alert, we have missiles that will actually be scored for the first time," he said. "We're not going to debate this. We're going to cheat to make sure we get reliable scores. All I want to know from the navigators is how to do this."

The senior navigator, who was also the bombardier, responded: "That's easy," he said. "Don't follow the missile needle. I'll figure out an adjustment for the ballistics, and I'll 'bomb' the target using my bombsight. All you have to do is ignore the missile's directions and follow the bombsight's needle, as we normally do. The tone is the same for the bombsight or the missile. The GCI site will not know that we're actually bombing the target. It will be simple, and no one will know."

Herb was shocked and speechless. As a West Pointer, he had been taught that you do not lie, cheat, or steal—or tolerate anyone who does. Some classmates terminated their own careers for the ideal of honor and integrity. This was expected. Honor and integrity were considered more important than success; there was no compromise under any circumstances.

Herb's crew was released from their duties after a week on ground alert. They had three days of time off with their families before getting together to plan the twelve-hour training flight with the missiles. The mission would include the simulated missile launch, some regular bomb runs, some navigation and bomb runs at low level, an aerial refueling, and a celestial navigation leg.

The three days were terrible for Herb. He was new to the crew and the squadron, but he had heard rumors that cheating sometimes occurred. Now he was being ordered to do it with the very missiles for which he was entrusted. He talked it over with other more experienced lieutenants in his squadron. They advised him not to rock the boat. They told Herb that cheating happened occasionally. If he refused to do this, they said, it would likely end his career.

Herb had worked long and hard to join the Air Force. He had studied hard for an appointment to West Point, and with difficulty managed to make it through his four years there. Herb had spent a year in navigation school, six months in bombardier school, attended Air Force survival training, and more weeks of B-52 ground and flying training. It had taken him six years altogether. How could Herb let it all slip away for this small act of cheating, which was apparently generally accepted? "I was taught integrity first and that this was the essential of being an officer and a leader. This lie was contrary to everything I had been taught and believed in," said Herb.

When Herb's crew met to plan the mission, he asked to speak to his aircraft commander privately. As soon as they were alone, Herb told him: "If you want to cheat, that's up to you. But get yourself a new navigator, because I'm not going to do it." Herb's commander was furious. The verbal abuse was extensive, and Herb was left literally shaking in his boots, thinking that his hard-worked-for career was at an end. After trying unsuccessfully to convince Herb to cheat, his commander left the room and slammed the door. Said Herb, "I was plenty scared, and I thought it was the end." He knew nothing about any other career to support his family. Plus, like today, there was a recession and jobs were scarce. The airlines had long since stopped using navigators, so even this wasn't a work option.

An hour or so later, Herb's commander was still angry and wanted to see Herb alone. Once alone he said, "Okay. We'll do it your way. But those missiles better be reliable."

"I'll do everything possible to make them so, but I won't cheat," responded Herb. He heard later that this commander told someone, "I don't know whether Herb's a good navigator or not, but I trust him. He's honest and he's got guts."

The missiles were reliable. Herb didn't know whether he was skilled, lucky, or his more experienced crewmates had found a way to fool their inexperienced young navigator and cheat anyway. One thing Herb did know. He knew how far he would go for what he believed to be right. He would go all the way. Out of 200 officers in his squadron, Herb was one of only three to eventually become a general.

I believe what I did then helped me immensely over the years, and it still affects my thinking today. Had it ended my career then and there, it still would have been worth it for this priceless piece of knowledge I now had about myself.

* * *

Over the years I have seen and worked with many leaders, in and out of the military. Some have demonstrated great personal integrity and gone on to great things. Others have demonstrated great integrity, and it cost them their careers. And yes, I have seen some with no integrity at all get promoted. But as I heard Peter Drucker say, although followers will forgive a leader much, they will never forgive him a lack of integrity. And as Shakespeare wrote: "This above all: to thine own self be true / And it must follow, as the night the day, / Thou canst not then be false to any man."

CHAPTER | ELEVEN

People Have No Limits

Ever wonder where the "Peter Principle" came from? Peter Drucker made it very clear that it did *not* come from him. The idea came from a best-selling book of the same title, written by academic Laurence J. Peter (along with Raymond Hull). Moreover, Peter (Drucker, that is) thought that the Peter Principle was badly mistaken, easily disproved, and likely to lead to serious problems at many levels of management if it were actually applied as presented.

Who Was Laurence J. Peter?

Dr. Laurence J. Peter was an associate professor of education at the University of Southern California. His best-selling book called *The Peter Principle* was published in 1969. The alliteration of the two *P*s helped the book catch on quickly. I rather suspect that its message resonated with many people because it implied that their bosses were incompetent. Peter's initial book was followed by several others on the same general topic. His central concept was that in a hierarchy, every employee tends to rise to his level of incompetence. Being incompetent at this level, the person then fails and is promoted no further—and would or should be removed from that position. If not, the organization suffers. It could even collapse, should the number of incompetents among its higher ranks reach a critical mass, resulting in the organization's inability to perform its functions efficiently, effectively, or competitively. Since demotion is usually not an option, it is probably best if the individual leaves the corporation.

Drucker's Take on the Peter Principle

Drucker didn't agree with this philosophy, although he thought Peter's theory was a highly innovative automatic-retirement sequence. Of course, he agreed that a nonperformer needs to be replaced. But he also believed that people have no particular limits, even after failure. This didn't mean that a manager should tolerate performance falling short of required standards; however, it did not mean that failure is necessarily the end of the line nor that the individual was incompetent—especially a proven manager who had done well in a variety of jobs previously.

Drucker also maintained that, all too frequently, the fault underlying the failure was a boss who put the individual in the wrong job. He told of a top executive who once reprimanded a vice president for wanting to fire a senior manager that same vice president had himself appointed. Previously that failing senior manager had years of success in the company. "The one thing we know for certain is that you made a mistake, since he was your appointment," the top executive told that vice president. Moreover, to fire this individual would not only be unfair, it would be stupid. "Why should we lose a proven manager as valuable as this individual, just because you made a mistake?"

Drucker felt that the Peter Principle was overly simplistic, that the demands placed on today's managers functioning at higher levels will likely lead to increasing failure rates, a phenomenon that has since been observed. Everything possible should be done to keep this failure from happening. "We have no right to ask people to take on jobs that will defeat them, no right to break good people. We don't have enough good young people to practice human sacrifice." He stated emphatically that selection of the right person for the right job was the supervising executive's responsibility. Incompetence could not and should not be tolerated. But before considering dismissal, consider the assumption that every failure is due to incompetence. There are many other possible reasons, including inexperience.

IBM Founder Declines to Fire Executive Who Blew $1 Million

There is a story that Thomas Watson, the founder of IBM, once asked to see a recently promoted vice president who had failed on his first assignment and cost the company $1 million. The young man reported to the IBM chief prepared for the worst; "I guess you called me in to fire me," he said, on entering Watson's office.

"Fire you?" exclaimed Watson. "We just spent one million dollars as part of your education."

A company that applies the Peter Principle puts significant additional pressure on its managers not to make mistakes, even though mistakes are an unavoidable part of business; there are always actions involving a reasonable balance of risk and potential advantage. This additional pressure, thus, is hardly conducive to developing a willingness to take risks or even assume full responsibility for actions, both of which are essential in good management. Such a "zero failure" climate inevitably creates problems. An organization that buys into and practices the Peter Principle is hardly encouraging its employees to perform at any level. It sends the message that long-term, hardworking, talented, and loyal employees must eventually and inevitably meet their fate: to be plummeted headlong out of the corporation, or at best be "kicked upstairs" or "put out to pasture" in a nonentity job. Accordingly, every manager at every level takes actions to ensure there are no mistakes, no failures. And this result yields an avoidance of reasonable risk, which leads to mediocrity and poor performance.

Round Pegs in Round Holes

Peter noted that implicit in the Peter Principle is the assumption that if managers are unsuited, or even incompetent for a particular job, they can't function well in any other job, at the same or at a higher level. This assumption is incorrect and therefore not only unfair but also incredibly wasteful of human potential. History is full of examples of "failures," of those who would be defined as "incompetent" under the Peter Principle, yet who later achieved great success.

Everyone knows the business Kentucky Fried Chicken, or KFC as it's known today. Colonel Harland Sanders had become a success with his fried chicken recipes long before he began wearing the white suits with bow ties, his goatee and mustache, and claiming the title of a colonel. He just made darn good chicken, which was noted by the then food critic Duncan Hines, and was even included as a mention in Hines's best-selling book, *Adventures in Good Eating*. However, the Colonel's restaurant suddenly failed—not owing to any particular incompetence on his part, but because a new interstate highway took the traffic away from his restaurant. At age sixty-five and destitute, Sanders took his monthly Social Security check and hit the road, seeking franchisees to sell the very tasty chicken prepared according to the recipe he had developed. His efforts were not immediately successful, and many would have said that he had reached his "level of incompetence." However, eventually Sanders did succeed such that, according to one story, he sold his fried chicken franchise company for a "finger-lickin' $15 million" only seven years later.[1]

Churchill's Rise from Failure

In some ways, Winston Churchill's story is even more impressive. Churchill was doing pretty well. He was a successful author and politician, and at the tender age of forty-one he became the First Lord of the Admiralty, a very senior position reporting to the prime minister, during World War I. With difficulty, he succeeded in convincing the British War Cabinet to undertake what turned out to be the biggest Allied seaborne operation of the war. However, Churchill had apparently reached his "level of incompetence" because this operation also turned out to be the biggest disaster of the war. This was the Dardanelles campaign, which included the catastrophic Allied landing at Gallipoli. It was a crushing defeat for the Allies, with over 200,000 casualties.

Churchill was forced to resign his job as First Lord of the Admiralty, and he was sent to the trenches in France as a rather junior lieutenant colonel commanding a battalion of infantry. Yet that same man was returned to his former position as First Lord of the Admiralty upon the outbreak of World War II. Then he was given much greater responsibilities when he was appointed prime minister upon the resignation of Neville Chamberlain. Winston Churchill saved England, and possibly the world, when the British stood alone against overwhelming odds and then went on to achieve victory over the Axis powers. Moreover, this "incompetent" is now considered the greatest British political figure of the twentieth century.[2]

Lincoln and Grant Also Failed Many Times

Politicians are great arguments against the Peter Principle. Abraham Lincoln failed in business; ran for the Illinois State Legislature and at first was defeated; went into business again and went bankrupt; ran for speaker of the Illinois State Legislature and was defeated; was defeated in his efforts to secure a nomination to the U.S. Congress; was rejected for an appointment for the U.S. Land Office; was defeated in a U.S. Senate race; and two years later lost the nomination for vice president at the first Republican National Convention.

Then, in 1860, he became our sixteenth president and he saved the Union. To the best of my knowledge, not even his detractors called him incompetent after that. Steven Spielberg's 2012 award-winning movie *Lincoln* showcased not only Lincoln's passion and persistence in convincing Congress to pass the 13th Amendment to the Constitution (which did away with slavery in the United States) but also displayed his competency and abilities as a politician and a president.

During the Civil War, Lincoln's general-in-chief, Ulysses S. Grant, was the only Union general who bested Confederate General Robert E. Lee on the battlefield. Earlier, Grant had been discharged from the army in disgrace for drunkenness, and then he had failed as a clerk in a retail store. Laurence J. Peter would have said that Grant had reached his level of incompetency with both failures and that he should certainly never have been named to a senior position, much less that of general-in-chief of the Union armies.

Peter's Principle

Drucker's belief in regard to the Peter Principle is that managers do *not* rise to their level of incompetence. If managers aren't performing, they need to be relieved of their duties. But to automatically fire a manager due to failure with no further thought is "human sacrifice," pure and simple. You don't waste individuals who have proven themselves over long periods of time, simply owing to a single failure, no matter how monumental. You find the right job for them. You keep in mind that people have no limits, even after failure.

Drucker's lesson is especially important at times when many good people are likely to lose their jobs owing to even minor errors—or maybe to cutbacks during an economic crisis, when they've made no mistakes at all. If you must do the cutting, ensure that the individuals let go fully understand that they may be far from reaching their "level of incompetence" and that a truly bright career may still lie ahead. And if you have the misfortune to lose your position yourself, understand that many very successful people have found themselves in your situation and have gone on to achieve much greater success.

2

Management

CHAPTER | TWELVE

Fear of Job Loss Is Incompatible with Good Management

According to Peter Drucker, outstanding performance is inconsistent with fear of failure in anything. He stressed this point in both his writings and his classes. Although his lectures were on management's need to take risks in decision making, they soon evolved into discussions on job performance and job security. In fact, Drucker's belief about this incompatibility between outstanding performance and fear of job loss would generate a firestorm of comments from his students. They went something like this:

- "You cannot ignore how your boss will react to your actions, even if ethically and technically they are correct."

- "Ignoring fear of job loss may be okay in theory, but it's a jungle out there. Disregarding the possibility you could be fired can lead to losing your job."

- "Fear of losing my job isn't the last thing I think of—it is the first thing."

Peter listened to these comments, but stuck to his earlier state-ment. "If you have this fear, you will improve your performance by learning to ignore it. Moreover, ethically it is what every manager must do."

What Happened When I Lost My Job

A few months after that class, I lost *my* job. I then knew exactly what my classmates meant when they thought fear of losing one's employ-ment was not to be dismissed lightly. I had conducted a successful, if somewhat unorthodox, job campaign some years earlier, when I had returned after several years abroad and had landed back home smack in the middle of a recession. At that same time, I had the added pres-sure of having to support a wife and two young children. It took seven weeks, but I got the job I wanted.

Buoyed by this prior success, I initiated a similar job search, in-corporating some additional insights I had gained from Drucker. Once comfortably employed again, I reflected on what had happened. Even before I completed my doctoral studies with Drucker, I began writing on how to conduct an executive job search. You might find some of these ideas useful.

Before You Lose Your Job, Prepare

You can minimize the fear of job loss and negate any effect it might have on your job performance if you are prepared for the possibility. Drucker was always an optimist; however, he was also a realist, and he prepared for contingencies. (Maybe that's why he was optimistic.) For him, the old concept of "expecting the best but being ready for the worst" applied. That didn't mean fearing the worst, but it did mean preparing for it.

Of course, while you're still on the job, you should work hard and take the right actions. That's expected of a good manager. However, no matter how solid your company or how well your boss thinks of you, you need to prepare for the potential loss of your job. How well I recall a friend telling me that his boss called his team together and said they would be untouched by the layoffs occurring throughout the company. A week later they were all let go, including his boss!

Maintain a Current Résumé

One of the best ways to prepare is to keep an updated résumé on your computer, organized around your specific work accomplishments. Note that I said "accomplishments," and not just experience. It is terrific that you had experience as a manager supervising over 100 subordinates, but what did you actually *accomplish* while in that position? Simply supervising people or having a certain title is insufficient. Did you increase the productivity of your organization by 25 percent? Did you or your organization win an award? Did you implement new methods that saved a significant sum of money?

You should keep a record of your accomplishments for every job you hold. And for those jobs you have held in the past, go back and include every past accomplishment as well. Quantify your accomplishments whenever possible, because quantified accomplishments are much more credible to a potential new employer. Be as specific and complete as you can be. And never mind whether the accomplishment involved a project lasting several years or only several hours. Something that you did and the experience you gained in doing it, even over a short period, are far more important than something on which you spent years. In fact, even a student looking for a first-time job has probably completed classroom projects or extracurricular activities that have direct applicability.

Start a Job Search

What if you are already out of a job and are reading these words? Then rework your résumé based on your accomplishments, not your experience. Your experience is the outline, or the bare bones, of your

potential—the potential to do future great things in a new environment. However, your accomplishments are the meat on those bones
and they make all the difference in your ability to land a great job in
the shortest time possible.

Having an up-to-date résumé is the most important part of
launching your job search when you are out of work. However, the
following four steps are also essential to getting any job search off on
the right foot.

Step 1: Ask Yourself What Business You Are In

Drucker recommended that all managers begin running their businesses or organizations with that question in mind. That's pretty
basic, but the implications are pretty profound and pretty important
for job finding, as well. Unless you decide that your former position
was totally out of your profession, don't go after any and every job
that happens to be open. Of course, if an opportunity comes along
you can consider the offer on its own merits. However, you can't be
everything to everybody, and trying to do so will only interfere with
your getting the best job that you can.

A potential future boss usually doesn't want "a jack of all trades."
He or she wants the very best, an "ace" in one trade, for one specific
job. Concentrating on what you have accomplished that supports your
likely future performance in a specific position should be the basis of
any successful job-search strategy. As a practicing manager, and once
as an executive recruiter, I've seen less qualified individuals preferred
by prospective employers and get jobs where others, some who were
much more experienced, were overlooked. Why? Because these other
job candidates didn't decide what business they were in, and they
didn't present their backgrounds as the *single* best candidate for that
single position. They tried to cover all the bases and show that they
had done a little something of everything. Candidates who may not
have done as much, but who focused on a single target, often got the
offer over those who did not.

Step 2: Cultivate Positive Thinking and Self-Confidence

Good jobs are scarce, but so are good candidates to fill them. That's why the executive recruiting field has blossomed in the last fifty years. You must believe that you are one of the top candidates out there looking for a job. You have to convince yourself that you have a lot to offer a potential employer. You can always look at the positive. During the Great Depression, the unemployment rate eventually hit a whopping 25 percent. That's pretty bad. However, if 25 percent of potential employees were out of work, that meant that 75 percent were working and had jobs. So positive thinking is always possible.

Positive thinking and self-confidence go together, and Drucker practiced both. Unfortunately, it is difficult to have either when you lose your job. If you have completed Step 1, then reread your résumé. This will boost both your positive thinking and your self-confidence, for unless you were a complete washout in your former jobs, you have some notable achievements that are of great value and will be impressive to your future employer. They will be impressive to you, too, as you read them over.

The current résumé on your computer is so important that you should read it regularly, update it, and add accomplishments as you remember them and as you conduct your job search. In this way, you will not only maintain your positive thinking and self-confidence, you also will know yourself better and appreciate what you have done in the past and can do in the future.

Step 3: Develop a Plan

You need to have a plan. You can't get "there" until you know where "there" is. Your planning starts with something you've already done—determining what business you are in, developing precise objectives, and creating a good description of the job you want, including the compensation, level of management, and geographical area. Of course, this process does not substitute facts for judgment, or as Drucker put it, "substitute science for the manager." However, systematic planning will strengthen your judgment, leadership, and vision and help you to focus on what you want and what you do not want.

Step 4: Work Your Plan

Your plan can be modified during your job-search campaign, but the important thing is to start. Your plan by itself won't get you anywhere. Drucker always insisted on action. He said that no plan was worth anything until it "degenerated" into work. In other words, Drucker didn't want you just to have a nicely developed plan. The plan had to be executed to have any impact at all.

* * *

Now that you know how to avoid fear from job loss, it's easy. Get started right away and develop your plan. Do everything but the implementation. Review and update your plan periodically. Do this, and sometime in the future when you may need to, you will rapidly find what you are seeking. Moreover, you won't fear loss of a job today, either.

CHAPTER THIRTEEN

You Can Accomplish
More with Less

Everyone knows that despite what leaders sometimes demand, you can't do more with less—or can you? I've heard it expressed as "you can't get blood out of a turnip." But many leaders of organizations have announced that "we must learn to do more with less." And in a surprisingly large number of cases, they went on to do exactly that.

I saw an economist on television discussing the difficulty in getting back the jobs lost during the recession. "In many cases," he explained, "companies have found that they didn't actually need the employees who were laid off. In other cases, they simply used the money they formerly paid the laid-off employees to accomplish the same jobs more efficiently and less expensively."

Long before the Great Recession, Drucker said you could do more with less and went on to prove it. This is done by reallocation of resources based on a discovery by and with a little help from a nineteenth-century Italian economist.

The Man Who Showed Drucker How to Do More with Less

Vilfredo Pareto was an Italian economist who, in the late 1890s and early part of the twentieth century, investigated the distribution of wealth in Italy. He found that roughly 20 percent of the population owned about 80 percent of the land. Strangely, this same breakdown held in a number of other populations that he investigated. Moreover, this breakdown was oddly consistent and predictable. Although Pareto's findings were published, not much was heard about this for many years. However, others began to notice the same, rather unusual pattern in many other areas of human endeavor. Most notably, these people included Harvard professor George K. Zipf, who discussed it in his Principle of Least Effort, and quality expert Joseph Juran, who proposed the Rule of The Vital Few.[1] Eventually it came to be thought of as a quirk of nature that holds true in regard to just about everything. Amazingly, roughly 20 percent of input causes roughly 80 percent of output or, stated another way, 80 percent of the results of anything comes from only 20 percent of the causative factor.

That is the secret of accomplishing more with less. Later, I'll show you how Drucker applied this idea directly to management. However, note now that this unusual breakdown is approximate—but close enough to catch the eye of a number of geniuses, including Peter Drucker.

Pareto in Your Daily Life

Pareto's phenomenon can easily be seen in your daily life. For example, you probably wear about 20 percent of the clothes in your closet about 80 percent of the time. This means that the money you spend for the 80 percent you rarely wear is largely wasted. Maybe you just like to see them hanging there, or you have a certain pride of ownership, or you feel more comfortable knowing that you have them to wear, if needed. However, the fact is, you could do more with less, a lot less if you had to. And the impression you'd make with your clothes will not change one iota, since you'd be wearing the same clothes as previously. Pareto's discovery began to be known as the 80/20 rule or the 80/20 principle, in which a majority of output results from a minority of input.

This has a significant effect in both your business and personal life. For example:

- 80 percent of your revenue comes from 20 percent of your clients.

- 80 percent of your HR problems are caused by just 20 percent of your employees.

- 80 percent of your company's customer complaints come from 20 percent of your products.

- 80 percent of your profits come from 20 percent of your products. Of course, 80 percent of your sales also are associated with 20 percent of your products, which may not be the same products. Both of these figures are important.

It is a basic principle of competitive strategy to concentrate your superior resources at the decisive point in the competition. The problem over the millennia has been to identify that decisive point. The 80/20 rule can help you do this. Drucker was clearly aware of this rule when he advised Jack Welch in his early decisions, which CEO Welch used to build General Electric into a $450 billion success story.

We'll see in Chapter 30 how Drucker operationalized Pareto's 80/20 rule with his concept of abandonment.[2] For now, if you want to do more with less, here's what you need to do.

1. *Regardless of what you are analyzing, find out where your results, good or bad, are coming from.* Let's say that you are using several different ways to sell your product or service. Some methods are so blatantly good or bad that the results are obvious. But in many cases, you need to look closer. In one business, I was surprised to learn that most contacts that led to sales were not coming from massive, varied, and costly methods of advertising but, rather, 80 percent of them were coming as referrals from personal contacts. Now

you probably already know that referrals are extremely effective—but 80 percent? Who would have thought?

2. *Remember, people are always important.* If there's to be a pruning, most companies just eliminate the troublemakers or those thought to be least effective at their jobs. But this type of thinking is no longer reliable or always true. For example, a sales engineer who was not the world's greatest dresser was thought to have poor interpersonal skills; it didn't help that he was almost always late to appointments. So he was scheduled to be first in line for layoff. There were no direct-sales metrics; it was an organization that didn't measure sales in direct numbers or dollars, as all the contracts were multimillion-dollar arrangements and involved several sales engineers assigned to the project. Fortunately for the sales engineer and his company, though, somebody noticed that this particular individual was associated with most of the winning contracts—about 80 percent of the wins. Closer analysis showed that he was going to extraordinary lengths in his interactions with customers, ensuring that their voices were heard on every project. This was unknown in the company and never considered before.

3. *Look closely at product for problems, complaints, and successes.* You'll be surprised at what you may find.

* * *

In summary, what you want to do is to model Drucker. He used Pareto and came up with the concept of abandonment. When adopted, this concept made a lot of money for a lot of companies. You can do the same.

CHAPTER FOURTEEN

What to Do About Office Politics

Office politics is the name we give to the negative and harmful maneuvering for position, power, status, and favoritism—or just plain love of the game-playing—that occurs to varying extents in many offices across the country and around the world. Office politics are difficult to control because organizations are made up of human beings with many different ideas, values, and personalities, and their ability and willingness to cause mischief varies widely as well. Worse, office politicians, whatever their goals, pay no entry fee and rarely incur a penalty for their participation. So there are few barriers to playing the game, and the cost to the individual for the actions may be very small. Unfortunately, the cost to an organization can be extremely high. That cost may include low productivity and poor performance, along with the loss or silencing of good people, whose voices need to be heard for the company to perform well. In the worst case, the cost may be the complete breakdown and failure of the organization.

Drucker's View of Office Politics

Drucker so detested office politics that he once gave it as his reason for avoiding faculty meetings, even though he and Dean Paul Albrecht were close friends who shared a passion for executive education. He stated his views on the subject at the very first class of executive Ph.D. students who met at the Faculty Club on the campus of Claremont Graduate School in Claremont, California. I was present as one of these students. This was a team-taught course in which both Drucker and Albrecht led the class for nine Ph.D. students. It was part of a controversial program intended to educate and prepare already successful executives, who possessed MBAs, for the top rungs of management in their companies.

This first course was intended as a no-holds-barred warm-up for the more rigorous courses and work to come. Though there was a written agenda, it was pretty loose. I don't recall how the subject came up, but Drucker reacted at once to the subject of office politics. In fact, he was uncharacteristically heated in his remarks. "Office politics can destroy any organization. You should avoid such things completely," he said. And then he added, "I do not attend Paul's [the dean's] weekly management meetings for precisely this reason." We all awaited a response from the dean. It was something to the effect of, "If you are Peter Drucker, you do not need to attend my faculty meetings."

In bringing Peter Drucker to Claremont, Paul had won out over several larger and then more prestigious graduate schools in the West that also wanted his services when he left New York University in 1970. They had offered more money and other incentives, but they could not match the executive program that Peter and Paul had envisioned. Now it was several years later, and this executive MBA program was well established. Peter had a lot of clout regarding what he would and would not do, including in this new executive doctoral program that I and the other eight had our eyes on. It may even have been in Peter's contract that attending faculty meetings was optional. In any case, we knew exactly how he felt about office politics. Though he wrote little explicitly about this topic, as his student I learned from him how to avoid and, if necessary, manage this destructive phenomenon. In view of this, consider that there are two perspectives from which a professional must view and manage office politics. Both require action, but of two different kinds.

The First Perspective: You Manage Yourself

Although a manager may be a supervisor, you are in an organization larger than that division or department, working in conjunction with other managers and thus in a universe subject to office politics over which you have little control. Yet, there is always one individual over whom every manager has control—himself.

Recently I was speaking with a well-known professional who knew Drucker well. Some years ago, this man was in an organization that was rife with office politics that he could not control. It was beginning to affect his attitude toward his work and toward his co-workers, and even, he thought, his ability to do his job. He explained the problem to Drucker and asked for his advice. Drucker responded, "The solution to your problem is simple, but not always easy to carry out: concentrate on your job, ignore the politics, and do not participate. Above all, just do your job."

Some years ago, a young man at a private college advanced rapidly up the career ladder. Hired as an assistant professor, the lowest rank on the academic ladder, he was quickly promoted to associate professor, and then to full professor. His obvious abilities led to his being offered the position of associate dean. In academia, administrative positions are a separate track that does not compete with the academic track of professors, who are supposed to focus on such activities as research, publication, teaching, and service. In fact, professors are treated almost as independent entities with great latitude in their activities. Nevertheless, administration is also important, and depending on the university, an associate dean, though sometimes viewed as a relatively junior position, is considered a stepping-stone to higher administrative posts, including dean, vice president, provost, and president.

The dean in this case was an older gentleman who had actually helped the young professor in his career at this university. However, becoming associate dean changed the young man. For the first time he was in a position to affect the entire School of Business. Moreover, he hungered for the deanship—so much so that he began to "play politics." He not only undercut colleagues who were potential competitors, he also began to talk behind the old dean's back and magnify to others any mistake that the dean made. Finally, he even tried to convince other professors to go to the president to recommend that the dean be removed from office and that he be appointed dean in his stead.

When these kinds of politics are afoot in any organization, the manager has no option. The offending "politician" must be removed from office. In this case, the associate dean needed to be fired. However, the dean did not act and the associate dean managed to destroy the dean's ability to lead. Too late, the president realized what was going on. The dean was forced to retire; much to the associate dean's surprise, however, a different dean was selected and he was moved to a staff position outside of the School of Business, where he had minimal contact with faculty. He received no more promotions.

To repeat Drucker's answer to my friend's query, "Above all, just do your job."

The Second Perspective: You Manage Others

As a manager, you cannot permit harmful office politics to rule in your organization; it is your responsibility to manage others. As noted above, the president failed to take action and thus lost an effective subordinate. But taking action is not always so easy. There is a hazy line between what is fair and good for the organization and what may be interpreted as favoritism.

Let's say one of your employees comes to you and asks for additional work. Is that office politics? If the individual is doing poorly dealing with the tasks you have already assigned him, the answer is pretty easy. But it's not so easy if this individual is in fact doing an outstanding job. Is it favoritism to comply with his request for more work? Probably not, especially if those you supervise could make the same request and, if deserving, have it granted. However, it is important that your policies are clearly known in advance.

The example of the associate dean seems clear enough when viewed here. But the harmful office politics he began should have been stopped by the university president, the dean's boss, before things had gone so far. Or the dean himself should have recognized much earlier that he had a growing problem from a scheming subordinate and have taken action, no matter how difficult this would have been or how much he might have preferred not to do so.

* * *

The best way for you as a manager to handle office politics is to make your policies clear and public. You can anticipate that some of your subordinates who are performing above average will seek additional work and responsibilities. Having everyone familiar with and understand your policies regarding promotion, selection for special jobs, additional work, and the like will go a long way toward heading off office politics or charges of favoritism.

What if, despite your best efforts, such harmful politics come into play? You need to stop them at once. Private one-on-one admonishment and announcements to everyone in your organization to cease and desist are your first steps, your initial lines of defense or, to be more accurate, your offense. If necessary, you will have to discipline office politicians or even remove them from the organization. They are that harmful and that destructive.

Drucker was no theoretician. He was a man of action. His recommendation was to take the action needed—don't let office politics destroy your organization.

CHAPTER FIFTEEN

Above All, Do No Harm

As I've mentioned earlier in this book, the ancient Greek physician Hippocrates came up with a cautionary note for physicians seeking to improve the state of their patients: "Above all, do no harm," or, if you prefer the Latin, *primum non nocere*. In a typical habit of taking something from one field and applying it to another, Drucker incorporated this phrase into his recommendations for the business manager. I suspect that he may have made the connection with consultants before he thought of applying it to all managers, since he himself was a practicing consultant and also because consultants are sometimes referred to as "business doctors." However, before we adopt this advice, it's well to understand from whence it came.

Hippocrates and His Do-No-Harm Theory

Hippocrates was a Greek physician born in 460 B.C. As Peter Drucker is known as the "Father of Modern Management," so Hippocrates is recognized as the "Father of Medicine." In the ancient world, Hippocrates was regarded as the greatest physician of his day. In the same way that Drucker looked at a business, Hippocrates looked at a patient and based his diagnosis on his observations. This was a breakthrough approach at the time. Hippocrates rejected the common view of his time that considered illness to be caused by evil spirits or the disfavor of the gods.

Drucker shared other features with Hippocrates's methods of observation and analysis. For example, Hippocrates believed that the human body must be looked at as a whole, not as individual parts to be analyzed, diagnosed, and treated separately. He was the first to accurately describe and catalog the indications of various illnesses. He developed the Oath of Medical Ethics, now known as the Hippocratic Oath, to guide physicians in their ethical and moral decisions. Many physicians today swear the Hippocratic Oath upon attaining the authority to practice their profession.

The statement "Above all, do no harm" is not included in the Hippocratic Oath, as I mentioned earlier in this book, but a close approximation of the phrase can be found in *Of the Epidemics*, also written by Hippocrates.[1] In this work, Hippocrates was cautioning that the physician must consider the possible harm that any intervention might cause. One could term such intervention unintended consequences, or a modern physician might call them side effects.

So, Drucker expanded this notion to mean that a leader must consider the possible harm that any action might cause to the mission, the organization, its members, or society. He considered this to be the ultimate guide for ethical conduct in business.

Failure to Follow This Rule Can Be Disastrous

Although a simple reading of Drucker's advice may give the impression that following this caution is easy, it is not so. Not infrequently, the well-intentioned acts of leaders can result in precisely what both Hippocrates and Drucker cautioned against. Sometimes the erring executive can deceive himself into thinking that he was clever, even skillful, when in actuality there was resulting harm done that was much greater than the intended good—sometimes even total calamity.

The Enron scandal is possibly the most notorious example of corporate misdeeds and ethical failure to have occurred in the last twenty-five years, and it came about because one well-educated, supposedly smart executive—CFO Andrew Fastow—thought he had found a way to enhance Enron's position through highly risky manipulations, concealing debts, exaggerating profits, and more. Fastow misled Enron's board of directors regarding these moves and he convinced the major accounting firm of Arthur Andersen to do likewise. The resulting disaster caused the collapse of the corporation, the closing of one of the country's leading accounting firms, the loss of thousands of jobs, and jail terms for many others. And you could even add the death of Enron's president, Kenneth Lay, who succumbed to a heart attack as he awaited sentencing.

It is hard to weigh these results against the supposed gain to the corporation. So while seemingly a simple rule to follow, like all simple rules, it is not always easy to implement. But failure to do so can have terrific, even catastrophic consequences.

Good Intentions Count for Naught

There are several ways that leaders can, with the best of intentions, cause harm to their organizations or to others and thus fall into this ethical trap. Most errors start with the intention to make some situation better. In many cases, the focus of the leader is so much on the good intention that the system as a whole is ignored and the unintended ancillary outcomes are overlooked or diminished. Drucker taught that good intentions were, of themselves, almost meaningless. It is all too common for these actions to have unintended negative impacts, all because this basic injunction was ignored.[2]

Example: A Good Intention Falls Afoul
of the Law of Unintended Consequences
Air pollution from motor vehicles has received a lot of attention over the last thirty years, and Drucker spoke about this in the classroom.

Environmentalists hurried to enact laws to help do away with this very real hazard. The solution was a device that would be affixed to the automobile to lessen the pollution caused by the engine's burning fuel. These devices work, but there is an unintended side effect. To eliminate, or at least reduce the pollution, individual states and the federal government passed laws limiting the amount of allowed emissions.

Probably an even more important factor in any overall reduction of emissions is the fluctuating price of gasoline, once 17 to 45 cents a gallon, then rising to as much as $4 to $5 a gallon, sometimes dropping a bit now and then. Most drivers preferred a higher performance car when gasoline cost but pennies. Yet despite laws, engine redesign, and high gas prices, at one point we had more air pollution produced by automobiles than before we started, even though U.S. standards, not to mention those of some states with very restrictive laws, exceeded those of many foreign countries.

True, many factors have been influenced by increases in the number of cars on the road, as well as the increased popularity of inefficient light trucks and sport utility vehicles in use, and the numbers of miles driven each day. However, this causal relationship ignores a basic, important element in Drucker's warning: Until technology eventually came to the rescue, the use of emissions-reduction devices on automobiles had an overall negative impact on the average miles per gallon achieved by these vehicles. So, if an average car is driven the same number of miles, it must burn additional fuel if an emissions-reduction device is added. Therefore, for a given number of miles, more gasoline must be produced to compensate for the effect of the pollution-control device.

More fuel needed to drive the same number of miles also translates to more oil needing to be refined into gasoline. However, it's not just a case of paying more for the miles traveled, or using up more of a scarce natural resource. The sad fact is that oil refining is a greater potential source of pollution than automobiles. With more refining needed, more pollution results. However, don't get the idea that I am against cleaning up the air. It's just that the solutions adopted sometimes make the problem worse—and this is such a case.

Example: Another Good Intention, Another Unintended Consequence

There's another example of how a law passed with good intentions has caused additional problems: water-saving toilets in the home. To help conserve water, some states have laws requiring that newly installed toilets use much less water per flush. (In California, commercial establishments are exempt, so they don't have the problem.) On the face of it, this sounds like a simple solution for problems of growing water scarcity. However, I sure noticed it some years ago when we put new bathrooms in our home.

Now, I've not bothered to do any scientific research on flush designs for these new toilets, but most people who use them say that they frequently need multiple flushes to eliminate waste. And our water bill supports the perception that these additional flushes have added to our water use rather than helped save water (although I've been told by one of my editors that it all depends on the toilet design). It could be I've just been unlucky. However, my point, again, is that for at least us unlucky ones we have a law intended to save water that instead ends up wasting it.

The problem can be that the attempt to make things better leads us to ignore the effect on the overall body or system. This falls under the classification of *primum non nocere* and it doesn't even depend on malicious manipulation by crooked managers.

Example: The Great Recession Started with Good Intentions

The roots of the recent mortgage crisis that contributed to the Great Recession go deep into the mid-1990s, and to the noble intention of making home ownership possible for more people. To accomplish this end, banking laws were eased and lending standards were lowered. Home mortgages were bundled and sold as investment securities. As a part of this effort, the Department of Housing and Urban Development (HUD) formulated policies that encouraged the issuance of increasingly risky loans, with at least 42 percent of the mortgages they purchased issued to borrowers whose household income was below the median in the area. Meanwhile, low interest rates further encouraged spending and investment. The idea that spending was "patriotic" was widely disseminated to encourage us to buy.[3]

The economy expanded and housing prices rose by double-digit percentages, with buyers assuming a continued rise in prices. Banking laws were further loosened, which permitted, and even encouraged, people to borrow money, not based on what they could afford but on how much they could spend. These practices also encouraged investors to borrow whenever and wherever possible in order to make money in a market that appeared to be a certainty for profits. In nine years, the number of subprime loans rose by 1,000 percent.[4]

It was always assumed that a lending bank cares about whether the loans it makes are repaid, and therefore it would carefully screen potential borrowers, regardless of hype. In the 1970s and 1980s and before that, this was in fact the case. The banks that originated mortgages usually held them over the long term and derived income from the interest paid as well as repayment of the principal. So banks would permit only those mortgages that were likely to be repaid—otherwise, they would lose money. However, new investment securities were developed that permitted banks to offload these obligations, thereby enabling them to make even more loans. For example, subprime mortgages could be broken into component parts, with the principal separated from the interest, and then both were packaged into securities with common characteristics, such as maturity or perceived risk, to be sold separately in financial markets.

These developments had a number of results that should have been foreseen as potentially harmful, but were not. The high yields at a time of low interest rates were very attractive to Wall Street investors, and these mortgage-backed securities developed quickly into a large market. Thus, the banks and mortgage companies no longer held the mortgages they originated; their main source of revenue was the origination fee, not the repayment of principal or payment of interest. As a result, the banks were no longer concerned about repayment, only with making as many of these loans as possible, under the very lenient lending laws that encouraged them to do so.

So the initial good intention of expanding home ownership and growing the economy ultimately created a toxic mix of incentives that ended when the bubble burst. Home values no longer continued to rise. In the recession that ensued, many new homeowners lost their homes, people who bought the mortgage securities were left penniless, and the general economy ground virtually to a halt.[5] Above all, do no harm? Many were harmed in this attempt to do good, which sooner or later would inherently lead to real harm when the real estate bubble burst.

And if one interjects human greed, which unfortunately but frequently clouds judgment when "everybody's doing it," a major disaster was inevitable. On one side, borrowers were encouraged to borrow money to purchase far more than they could afford. It seemed that they couldn't lose! They would make money on the deal as housing prices continued to soar. Lenders were encouraged to approve as many mortgages as possible, since the market was so overheated they could sell the mortgages in these investment packages before any repayment problems would arise, even those of clearly risky borrowers. But remember—this all started with a good intention: to enable more Americans, especially poorer citizens, to own their own homes.

Keep Drucker's Advice in Mind

If you really want to implement Drucker's injunction to "above all, do no harm," do the following:

- Remember, good intentions don't count for anything.

- Beware of unintentional results and analyze bad things that could happen, because they often will.

- Look before you leap, especially with new concepts and untested ideas.

- Don't be seduced into doing something because "everyone is doing it."

CHAPTER SIXTEEN

How to Avoid Failure

What I am about to say sounds counterintuitive. In fact, it *is* counterintuitive. But Drucker showed us that it is absolutely true, nonetheless. Peter Drucker found that if you continue doing what made you successful in the past, you will eventually fail. This has been true in all times and in every field, including not only business but also war, politics, and even sports. Companies, industries, and countries that have failed to understand this single principle make up the scrap heap of history. What is this one principle that will help you to avoid failure? Let me put it to you straight: Stop doing what made you successful!

Even Experienced Generals Have Trouble with This Lesson

World War I was fought in trenches, and the more formidable the trench defense, the more difficult to move forward. After four years of this, the participants all became proficient in this way of making war. The conflict was fought mainly on French soil, and the French were determined that this would never happen again. World War I trench warfare taught them the value of static defensive combat and exactly what needed to be done to make impregnable their border with their traditional enemy, Germany.

Under the direction of Andre Maginot, the French minister of war, France built what military experts around the world agreed was a work of genius. It consisted of a supertrench extending along the German border, with concrete fortifications connected by tunnels and with machine-gun emplacements, tank traps, artillery positions, and more. Soldiers were totally protected and safe from bombardment, sheltered not only by concrete but also by being housed underground. The world had never seen anything like it. It was impenetrable against direct attack. Nevertheless, the Germans easily defeated it in World War II. They simply went around the Maginot Line and attacked the French army through Belgium. So fast was their advance that a new name, blitzkrieg, or "lightning war," was given to this new form of warfare. They stopped doing what had succeeded in the past and did something new.

Failures in Business

In recent years, we've seen failures of financial organizations so powerful we would never have thought it possible. Lehman Brothers, AIG, Merrill Lynch, Fannie Mae and Freddie Mac, Washington Mutual, and many others have collapsed, been bailed out by the government, been acquired by others, or are coping with serious problems brought on by their failures. Unfortunately, hundreds of other formerly successful organizations, big and small, are proceeding down the same primrose path to failure, in blissful ignorance that disaster awaits just around the corner.

This is not only a result of a recession. I'm talking about organizations that aren't in danger now. They are the ones that plan to operate following the same, successful ways as in the past. Drucker would say that they're making a big mistake.

The failures in the recent financial crisis are rightfully assigned to the catalysts that brought it on: derivative loans gone bad and the collapse of the housing industry. Yet those financial organizations might have seen the danger ahead. They could have taken Drucker's advice and changed course before it was too late. They might have seen that the situation was too risky, given the fact that any business boom will eventually go bust. They could have gotten out. Most didn't.

You can find all sorts of companies that could and should have introduced new products and services to replace their successful ones, but failed to do so. New technologies always supplant the older ones, so they shouldn't be ignored. The railroad, one of the great inventions of the nineteenth century, helped develop the American West and in the process created some of the wealthiest men in America. Yet by World War II, it was clear that air travel, superhighways, and buses would cut into the railroad's monopoly.

Marketing experts say it was a question of business definition. They say that the successful old-line companies, the B&O, the Union Pacific, the Atchison, Topeka and Santa Fe, and many others simply thought they were in the railroad business, when in reality they were in the transportation business. Had they given it deeper thought and defined their businesses properly, maybe we would have a Union Pacific Airline today.

Surely the ubiquitous slide rule, once carried by engineers worldwide, might have been easily identified as a candidate for immediate replacement once the handheld calculator came on the scene. I could go on, but you get the idea. The point is, like a lightbulb that burns its brightest just before complete failure, many companies and industries are at their best just a few years—or in some cases, just a few months—prior to their bankruptcy.

Unexpected Failures Have a Common Cause

Why do these unanticipated failures occur? Because the companies continued to blindly do what made them successful in the past. Why *can't* a company or organization continue to do what has made it successful? Because the environment changes in some critical way that invalidates the old rules. Maybe it's technology—something new like the automobile comes along and downgrades the horse from a means of transportation to a sport or pastime. Or it could be economics— the economy falls into depression or becomes inflationary. The first condition might cause potential customers to hold on to their money; the latter might cause them to spend more freely and in a much shorter period of time.

Frequently, it is social change that makes the difference. Bathing suits covering the entire body go out of fashion, but swimwear makers stick with what they know. Meanwhile, the bikini covers only a few square inches (the French inventors had to hire a nude cabaret dancer to model it in 1946, but today it's a billion-dollar a year industry). Prior to the 1950s, almost all men wore hats. Now, men's hats have been relegated to a few specialty stores.

You can't ignore politics, laws, or regulations, either. What was once legal can become illegal and vice versa. Prohibition of the sale of alcoholic beverages becomes illegal, or becomes legal (both happened in the 1920s in the United States), and causes major changes in the spirits industry, not to mention criminal behavior.

What about new actions by competitors? A competitor can become successful in an action that you have not anticipated. That's where the French failed with the Maginot Line. Apple Computer started the personal computer industry, but IBM's strategy of encouraging rather than restricting others in making compatible software gave IBM PCs the edge.

There are all sorts of other unexpected major events, from earthquakes and storms to acts of terrorism. The terrorist attack on September 11, 2001, led to increased air travel restrictions and much greater security. As a result, there's been more talk of virtual meetings using new technologies including super-high-definition, three-dimensional electronic imaging.

The Future Cannot Always Be Easily Anticipated

Drucker gave us some good ideas on how to predict the future, but he said that the best way was to create the future ourselves. You might think senior leaders can easily anticipate and readily prepare for change. But this is rarely the case, for several reasons. These leaders have been successful because they were effective under the old paradigm. Their own and their organization's prior actions made them and their companies successful. So, they are comfortable with the old way, hesitant or not open to some new, unproven ideas or ways of doing business. Some are afraid to deviate, afraid to make a mistake. They invested heavily in the old model and they want to avoid anything that indicates they must invest again or start over. It takes an exceptional leader to decide to make the change, or even to utter words implying that change will be necessary.

Of course, there is a challenge involved in adopting Drucker's counterintuitive advice. It would be foolish, even dangerous, to abandon successful products, organizations, strategies, or weapons systems while they are still profitable and useful. How, then, can you recognize that significant change is near? How do you know when to take action with your products, services, or means of operating so as to be ready? Here are a few suggestions:

- Keep your eyes open and know what's going on. Familiarize yourself not only with new products but also with anything else that could remotely affect your operations. This means a steady regimen of reading trade journals, newspapers, and other relevant media. Drucker said his ability to predict the future was possible by simply thinking about events that had already happened, and what changes these events would cause in the future.

- Play a "what if" game with yourself. What would you do if . . . ?

- Watch trends and new developments closely. If sales drop over several quarters, find out why. Do not automatically assume that everything will "return to normal." There is no normal.

- Face facts. Nothing lasts forever, so prepare yourself mentally for change and take action when necessary, regardless of your previous investment in time, money, or resources. He who hesitates is lost!

- Don't do things differently just for the sake of doing so, but establish a program of continual review for every product, strategy, tactic, and policy.

- Aggressively see change as an opportunity to stay ahead of the competition. That's what Ford did when sales of its Falcon were faltering. They noticed that certain options such as the four-on-the-floor and the padded dash were increasing, so they introduced the Mustang, which gave them a multiyear lead over the competition.

- Never be afraid to obsolete your own products, services, and strategies, and look for better ways to meet the demands, wants, and needs of your customers.

Do these things and you'll not only stay ahead of the competition, you'll survive and succeed brilliantly while others, plodding on in the old way, will falter.

CHAPTER SEVENTEEN

Quality Is Not What You May Think

Every organization says it has "quality," but just saying you have it isn't enough. Quality is a necessary and important part of any product or service you offer, whether that product or service is an automobile or an airplane, a potential candidate for a job, or the due diligence conducted by a consultant, attorney, or accountant prior to an acquisition. The word also reflects what *you* mean by quality. But do you ever think about what quality means to your *customer*?

For instance, the speed at which you provide your service is likely part of quality, either as seen by you or your customer. However, is this speed fast or slow? In a fast-food restaurant, most customers want the pace of service to be fast. On the other hand, customers in a fancier restaurant will prefer a slower pace, especially if they are conducting a business meeting or the meal is part of a romantic evening.

Quality is indeed a relative matter. I was making a presentation to a potential corporate client a few months ago, proud that the program we had developed would aid students in completing a demanding MBA program in only eleven months, rather than the standard two years—what I viewed as a quality improvement. "You don't understand," the vice president of human resources said. "We don't want our employees to complete their MBAs that quickly. They'll get their MBAs and then leave us. We want them to take at least two years." So, there are many different ways of looking at quality, but you should *always* view it from the point of view of the customer.

You Think You Got Quality? It Ain't Necessarily So

According to Drucker, quality in a product or service is not what the supplier puts into it. It is what the user gets out of it. It's what they pay for.[1] Users want only what they can use and what gives the product or service value for them. I emphasize "for them." Value is as they perceive it, and quality is part of that value. Therefore, it is foolish for a seller to spend money, time, and effort developing quality as he sees it, for the buyer may not see it that way at all. Further, it is equally foolish to promote durable products that will last forever, or products or services that are provided fast, or even products that are 100 percent reliable in manufacturing, if these features are not what is desired or appreciated as value by the user.

I once worked for a company that made oxygen breathing masks for military aviators. It supplied the masks to the government in quantities of upwards of 40,000 at a time. Many other companies had tried, but none had ever succeeded in getting into this market. That was because of a single valve that was used in the oxygen mask. No matter how much "quality" the other manufacturers built into the valve, a significant number of valves would fail to perform as specified during quality testing of production batches. In fact, the more bells and whistles that were added, the more difficulty the company had in meeting the specifications of the test. And those "high-quality" valves the competitors offered were made of expensive and exotic materials, frequently making those products far more expensive than those manufactured by my company. The government couldn't have cared less about added gimmicks; passing the test was absolutely critical, though.

Moreover, it turned out that testing a percentage of valves off the production line in any batch was meaningless. Unfortunately for the competitors, there were still always a significant number of valves that would fail their quality control test. Yet my company always had a 100 percent success rate on our valves. What was our secret?

Though well-guarded, the secret wasn't complicated at all and didn't require a "higher-quality" valve. Our success rate for production of the valves wasn't any better than the competitors'; in many cases, our success rate may actually have been worse. But my company realized that the government didn't care whether or not the valves were consistent in meeting production standards.

Quality for the government was whether the valves *delivered* met quality standards in the test, not whether the company could consistently produce a valve that met these standards. In fact, our production chief told me that he didn't think anyone could produce valves such that every single valve in a batch met the quality specs. Yet, except on very rare occasions, every single valve that my company turned over to the government easily passed the government specifications. How did we do it? The solution was simple, but unheard of. We didn't test a percentage of valves in a batch to ensure reliability; we tested every single one of the valves sent to the government, whether that involved 40 or 40,000 valves. Those that failed were simply tossed out. This was a much more expensive procedure than if production could develop a valve that could consistently pass the test after production, but it fulfilled the customer's definition of quality, and this was Drucker's point.

Another Kind of Quality

Drucker was not recommending that suppliers offload poor workmanship or performance because that's what the user supposedly wants. This is a defense one hears occasionally from some suppliers, such as publishers, television producers, newscasters, or those in other similar industries as to why "quality" products are no longer provided: "We're just giving people what they want." No, that's an excuse for low quality. But how can quality be measured? And can it be quantified in order to be measured?

Sometimes, quantity may be a part of quality. For example, the quality of a surgeon's work can be quantified by the number of operations he performs annually. That may be important to a for-profit health-care provider paying a number of high-priced physicians. But except under emergency conditions, the quantity of operations a doctor performs is not important; rather, it's the number of operations performed *successfully*. This is a different kind of quality, the quality of performance or productivity, as opposed to a benefit, value, or feature.

While one might quantify, and thus measure, performance or productivity even with knowledge workers, this is not the major problem. The major problem is the difficulty in deciding which task of the job should be measured. Look at the wrong task in the product or service, and you get the wrong answer. Drucker demonstrated this with a prime example: public schools in the inner city.

Measuring Quality of Performance and Productivity

By most measures, inner-city school systems cannot be considered a success story. Yet right next to them, in the same geographical areas and in the shadow of the same conditions of crime and poverty, there often are successful private schools. These are not private schools in the sense of boarding schools or schools catering to the wealthy or the elite. Most of these are religious schools, and even though the parents of the attendees are not wealthy, they scrape together enough money to send their children to these schools or they earn scholarship admissions.

The students come from similar backgrounds as the students going to the inner-city schools, yet the contrast in school results is noteworthy. Yet while the public schools next door complain of indifferent students, crime, and lack of discipline, the atmosphere in these other schools is the opposite. I saw this myself when, as an Air Force general, I was asked to attend the ceremony at which several high schools in inner-city areas received their official acceptance as junior Air Force ROTC units. I found high standards and the kind of discipline any West Pointer would be proud of, right in the midst of some of the most dangerous neighborhoods.

According to Drucker, while there were many reasons for the differences between these two classes of schools in the same areas, the primary one is how each defines its mission. Most inner-city schools see their mission as helping the underprivileged. The private schools define their task as "enabling those who want to learn, to learn."[2] Does how a school defines its mission influence the quality of its product? You bet it does!

A professor I knew who was teaching at a state university once contrasted output as he saw it at his school with that of a more prestigious school in the same geographical area. Both schools offered similar degrees and both were accredited by the same accrediting bodies using the same standards. Both required their professors to do research and to publish, although the more prestigious school encouraged its professors to publish more and in journals of higher quality. However, the state school's tuition was about a third of that of the more prestigious school. Moreover, the state school defined its primary mission as teaching the first generation of a family to attend college.

This professor made an observation that I found fascinating. "They [the prestigious school] teach success," he said. "At my school, we teach survival." Accurate definitions of one's tasks are essential in the production of any product or service, and these definitions affect the resulting observed quality output.

Is Quality a Condition or a Restraint?

Work performance translates to quality for many jobs, and therefore performance also describes the output produced. Moreover, quantity produced may be secondary to quality.[3] Yet, a simple comparison of quality versus quantity is not reasonable. There are jobs for which both quality and quantity define performance, and thus task definition. Sales jobs may be one example. An unfortunately large number of organizations define a salesperson's performance in terms merely of quantity—so many units sold, or such and such number of dollars brought in. This rather limited definition of performance needs careful analysis.

Years ago, there were two tired salesmen seated next to each other on a train, riding home after a hard day's work. After identifying to one another that both were in sales, one asked the other, "How did it go today?"

"Not so bad," responded the other. "I took wholesale orders for over twelve dozen men's shirts. How about you?"

"I sold two," answered the first salesperson.

"Oh, too bad," his new friend commiserated. "I'm sure you'll have a better day tomorrow."

"It wasn't a bad day, it was one of my best," replied the salesman whose sales were so few. "I sell airplanes."

However, even this simple example doesn't begin to explain the complexity of defining quality, especially for sales performance. Some very adept salespeople, whose dollar and quantity figures may be quite satisfactory, fail in the long run by not properly servicing the accounts to whom those sales were made. They then hurt the company or the brand's good name and ultimately lose future sales to the competitors. They, or their managers and higher-ups, have overlooked the fact that it is far easier and less expensive to obtain sales from established customers than to find and convert prospects into new customers.

Quality Requires a Different Way of Looking at Things

Drucker knew to look at quality in a product or service in a different way. We have to see it not as what we think is right and good, but as the customer views it. Only the customer can truly define what quality is, what the customer considers of value and can use, and therefore what is important to consider in a purchase. Once we get that right, we can measure performance and productivity in that area. We can then factor in features that the customer may not be aware of. Only in this way can we get the definition of quality right. And only then can we claim that we provide quality.

CHAPTER | EIGHTEEN

Implementation Requires Controls

Our astronauts on their voyage to the moon were rarely on course. No, it wasn't that we picked poor navigators or that we did not train our astronauts well. But space navigation is immensely complex and the calculations are far from easy. First, both Moon and Earth are moving bodies. That's like taking off from Los Angeles during an earthquake to land in New York, which has lost its connection to the continent and is drifting away while rotating. Fortunately, the gyrations of both Earth and Moon are not random, and astronauts can predict how Los Angeles's gyrations have affected the spacecraft's course as it was thrown into space on takeoff, and where New York City's wanderings would take it by the time of the spacecraft's arrival. However, it's critical that the astronauts know three things about their spacecraft with certainty:[1]

1. Where the spacecraft is in space and where it is going

2. Which way it needs to go to stay on or return to the planned path

3. How and when to fire its thrusters to match the planned path

To sum up, they need to know where they are, they need to know where they are going, and they need to have controls that allow them to correct their course during implementation of the flight.

That is, someone needs to take action for the implementation of space flight—or for anything else, for that matter.

Action Is Required

Yes, action is required for implementation. Drucker wrote that the best plan is only a plan, merely good intentions, unless it "degenerates" into work. Of course, his use of the word *degenerate* was meant to be humorous, since it connotes a less desirable state from previously. He chose the word because he saw that plans often degenerated in the minds of people who have trouble going from planning to action. Aside from the humor, it is absolutely true that without action, nothing is achieved. This is true in space navigation, and it is true in business, marketing, and life.

How many talented professionals have you known who excelled in producing great ideas, but lacked follow-through? As a result, the jobs never got done. They may have even turned the switch on by telling others to begin, but then they just let things run downhill. Their ideas may have begun moving in the direction they were intended, with no updating or oversight. Or, even that might not have happened. The action might have stopped shortly before it was begun.

This happens because no attempt was made to ensure that the initiated actions were carried out to completion. No attempt was made to discover whether everything was working out as intended, whether the future was being shaped as envisioned, or whether the actions should be modified or even changed drastically in order to reach the intended goal.

In failing the critical task of follow-through, the planner wasted the time, effort, and resources of all the work that had been invested. The planner failed to establish and use *controls*. I doubt many of our astronauts' voyages would have been successful had they neglected the controls. Even unmanned missions require controls.

Controls: The Key Ingredient for Successful Implementation

As with any project, a great idea needs to be managed. Management requires a breakdown of tasks, assignments as to who is to do what, time schedules, resource allocations, performance expectations, a means of measuring results, periodic and ad hoc reviews, and feedback. To do this, you must have controls. According to Drucker, controls have three major characteristics:[2]

1. Controls can be neither objective nor neutral.

2. Controls need to focus on results.

3. Controls must consider measurable events, but also those that are not measurable.

Neither Objective nor Neutral Be

No matter how scientific we try to be, when we control something we induce error in measurement. Since we need to measure the effect of an action, this characteristic is of some importance because the very act of establishing the control creates focus and can influence the results.[3]

The most famous (or infamous) example of the errors that can be induced through controls was a study done at the Hawthorne Works in Cicero, Illinois, beginning about 1924. An experiment was set up to measure productivity improvement with better illumination of the work area. Not surprisingly, it was found that by increasing the wattage of the electric lightbulbs under which the workers performed their duties, productivity increased. All well and good. However, the productivity continued to improve even though the wattage was increased only slightly. Suspicious, the investigators decreased, rather than increased, the wattage of the lightbulbs. Surprise, surprise—productivity still increased! This became known as the Hawthorne effect, identified as such in 1955.

The attention paid to the workers during the experiments is what caused a short-term increase in productivity. The Hawthorne effect has been observed many times, in different settings and environments. The results are still controversial, as they have not always been replicated.[4] But similar results have been obtained in other experiments.

Controls Must Focus on Results

The major difference between a manager and a leader, according to Drucker, is that the manager focuses on doing things right, while the leader focuses on doing the right things. This is not a simple play on words. Of course, we all like a leader who is both efficient (doing things right) and effective (doing the right things). But if it is a choice between the two, and this determines focus, then the leader must focus on the latter: getting the right job done, whether the job is performed efficiently or not.

In my opinion, this was the great weakness of the Total Quality Management (TQM) movement, even though it had many good attributes, including ownership, continuous improvement, empowerment, and high quality. However, TQM focused on process rather than results. The theory was that if you had the most efficient process in place, the best result would just naturally follow. Unfortunately, as demonstrated by many organizations that adopted TQM, this is not necessarily true.

The Florida Power and Light Company, winner of Japan's Deming Prize for quality management, abandoned TQM owing to worker complaints within a year. The Wallace Company, a Houston oil supplier, won the prestigious Malcolm Baldrige National Quality Award and went bankrupt shortly thereafter.[5] The control system you use for your implementation must focus on goals and intentions, not just gaining efficiencies along the way.

Measurable and Nonmeasurable Events

Controls are needed for both measurable and nonmeasurable events. Drucker's concern was that measurable events would gradually overshadow nonmeasurable results, yet the latter are frequently more important. His example of a critical nonmeasurable event, or at least one that is not normally looked at, is the *need* for an organization to attract and hold able employees.[6] However, while the *need* to attract and hold able employees may not be measurable, measurements designed to calculate how an organization is doing in meeting this need can easily be developed. These might measure employee satisfaction, employee turnover rates, time needed to acquire new hires, and so forth.

Control Requires Metrics

The measurements necessary for control are frequently termed "metrics." Choosing the correct metrics and making the decisions about them are incredibly important in their use for control, in both the day-to-day and the strategic sense. Choice of the wrong metrics, or if their collection is organized or analyzed incorrectly, can lead to a multitude of problems while failing in their purpose of rendering control.

Here's an example of the curious results that can be obtained from measuring the wrong things. A large Air Force command established a management control system and performance measurements were developed for important aspects of the unit's primary mission and support functions. One of the support functions at most U.S. military installations, both then and now, consists of social club–like organizations where members can eat, drink, and play—much like the country clubs and golf clubs used by corporations for this purpose.

All of these clubs are for the benefit of members and their families and guests, and are supported by the members, not by the government. Membership is voluntary, although there is some pressure to participate. The result is that almost everybody joins and pays a modest monthly membership fee. These clubs offer one or more restaurants, a swimming pool, services like check cashing, and usually pool and ping-pong tables, as well as a place where everything from bingo and bridge clubs to parties and weddings could also be held.

Since club membership fees are intentionally kept very low, like many civilian restaurants, a disproportionate amount of income comes from the bars, which tend to ensure profitability for the club. These clubs are not set up to be profit centers, but to serve their members. Usually any profits generated are turned back to the club, and the elected club board makes the decision as to how to distribute these funds to less profitable club activities.

In this one Air Force command, it was decided at the higher level of authority that the basic metric for all the clubs would be profit. One club's profits would be compared with another. The metric was not, however, overall club profit, but profit for each part of the club. For example, the swimming pool never charged fees. The costs for maintenance of the pools, lifeguards, and such were all covered by surplus funds from the bar. The restaurant provided exceptionally good service and high-quality food at low prices. These, too, were enabled due to the profitability of the club bar.

The new management control system, whereby each department of the club had to demonstrate profitability, created immediate problems. The swimming pools had to charge fees for use. Use therefore declined. The restaurants could no longer offer the same quality of food or service. As a result, they were no longer competitive with many nearby civilian restaurants. In desperation and in trying to become profitable, some clubs turned to highly questionable cost-cutting practices. One club ceased purchasing catsup and mustard bottles. Instead, the small government-issue tubes of catsup and mustard, when unused, were salvaged from flight lunch boxes after an aircraft mission. Club members deserted the club restaurants and soon membership declined.

Only when metrics based on service as well as profits were reinstalled did the clubs return to their previous state. The point: You must use the correct metrics and draw the correct conclusions from the data.

Drucker's Nine Control Specifications

There are nine specifications for an effective control.

1. Economical and not unduly costly

2. Important to the intended outcome

3. Appropriate to what is being measured

4. Appropriate to the events being measured

5. Timely

6. Uncomplicated

7. Actionable

8. Reviewable both periodically and on the spur of the moment

9. Accountable for results

Follow these nine specifications as Drucker recommended and proper implementation of your plans is ensured.

CHAPTER NINETEEN

Do the Right Thing at the Right Time

Marcus Junius Brutus, best known to us simply as Brutus, was the statesman who uttered the words: "There is a tide in the affairs of men,/Which, taken at the flood, leads on to fortune." At least, he did this in Shakespeare's play *Julius Caesar.* As events would later prove, Brutus may have been correct about the tide's existence, but he must have missed taking it "at the flood," since his participation in the assassination of Caesar didn't lead to fortune, but to his eventual suicide a little over two years later. Drucker would have agreed completely that such a tide exists, and would probably have gone further to suggest that timing is mightily important even for, or maybe especially for, an assassination and in the management of the events that follow. So, too, are activities in modern times heavily dependent on doing the right thing at the right time.

Timing Can Be Wrong, for Different Reasons

Some years ago, an entrepreneur established a web design and hosting company. He understood the importance of marketing segmentation, and he decided that, owing to his background and experience, he knew independent CPAs best. Unfortunately, he had not assimilated either Shakespeare's or Drucker's lessons on timing. To his chagrin and loss of income, his timing selection of the middle of March to run a direct-mail campaign to sell something to CPAs was unfortunate. After spending lots of money and getting few leads for his business, this web entrepreneur finally figured out that, since his prospects were in the middle of tax season, they were too busy doing taxes to consider his proposition.

This was an example of trying to do something when the time was not right. The web designer reorganized his plans and spent his scarce remaining resources to promote his service to CPAs at a more favorable time of year. It was still the wrong time, for an entirely different reason this time around. Too few CPAs were familiar with web advertising; and it probably wouldn't have worked in attracting their customers either, since the explosion of online search engines was still early and many prospects were not yet online. So, even when his prospects had the time to read and consider his advertising material, the entrepreneurial web designer lost money again.[1] Fortunately for him, he was able to re-relaunch his company shortly thereafter, poorer but wiser with the knowledge that timing is not an insignificant factor!

Drucker on the Importance of Timing

Drucker recognized that timing was everything for all management actions. There are two major problems in timing that he thought were unique to management. Both result in additional challenges for decision makers. The first is that the time for development is lengthening for many products that constitute completely new technologies. He pointed out that, in the 1880s, Thomas Edison spent no more than fifteen months from product conception to product introduction for many products that didn't exist previously. However, to develop similar products over a hundred years later—the lightbulb or the motion film projector, for example—might take fifteen years for a similar cycle of conception to introduction in the marketplace. Remember, it's not just thinking up and developing the product; if the market for it doesn't already exist because the public is not yet familiar with the product and its use, this can take much longer than you might expect. This is probably even more true of intellectual property.

I was once asked at an academic conference why it took more than thirty years before a common practice today—the routine preparation of a marketing plan—became institutionalized at most U.S. corporations. I pointed out that, assuming the marketing plan followed standard practice after the initial idea, it would first be applied and tested. Research would be conducted on its efficacy and submitted to one of the academic journals. To get published in such a journal commonly requires peer review—the opinion of experts—and often revision. This review and revision process can take several years. Unfortunately, these academic journals are read by few practitioners.

After publication in the journal, the next step is for that idea to be taken up by a textbook author in the field, who likes the idea and references it in a new edition. This, too, requires some years. When the textbook gets published, and assuming it is popular, it gains sufficient adoptions by professors around the country and then many students learn the process. However, these students are not yet in positions of responsibility. So, there's a minimum of another ten years before a new idea, such as routinely doing a marketing plan, becomes a popular concept. Of course, there are ways to shorten this process, but you get the general idea.

If the new product is one subject to regulation, such as drugs, government agencies are involved and that extends the trial period even longer. And today, not only drugs are regulated. As someone pointed out, even the Wright brothers might not have been allowed to fly their airplane without government approval, since the concept was unproven until they did it.

The second major problem in timing is that technological development is causing the obsolescence of products at a much faster pace. The electric handheld calculator was the size of a small brick when first introduced in 1972. It was a bargain at close to a hundred dollars, even though it had no memory function. Less than five years later, it had shrunk to the size of a credit card and was selling for less than five dollars—and today it is not infrequently given away as a promotional item. Additionally, the giveaway has a lot more functions than "the brick," including a memory. The same is true with products introduced more recently. How many new smartphones, iPads, or other high-tech products do we go through in relatively short periods?

Example: An Almost Secret Birth and a Rapid Demise

Federal Express, or FedEx today, has had a number of highly successful services. Zapmail was not one of these. It was withdrawn even before it got warmed up. Zapmail was well named and did provide what was a valuable service at the time. It delivered faxed messages for business clients before the general availability of fax machines and when they were still pretty pricey. For high-volume users, there was an added option. FedEx would install its own fax machines on the client's premises with the electronic transmission being carried over the FedEx private network. The company's investment and the charges to the corporate customer were both relatively high, or would be considered so today. But FedEx believed in its investment and thought the cost was worth it for many customers to see their material delivered within hours rather than overnight. At the time it was conceived, this assumption was probably valid. In fact, at that time the project was so hot it was kept secret and carried the code name Gemini.[2]

However, quality problems caused delays. Even the loss of the space shuttle *Challenger* played a role, since it caused FedEx to abort the planned incorporation of final transmission by satellite. The clock was ticking. By the time these and other problems were resolved, the cost of fax machines had fallen considerably. Meanwhile, relatively few customers had signed on. When FedEx dropped the project only two years after its introduction, losses were in the neighborhood of $320 million.[3] Again, timing, even if it's not the fault of the innovator, rules the endeavor.

Timing for the Present and the Future

A challenge that innovators always face in timing is that they must make decisions considering not just the present but also the future. Or, as Drucker put it, a management decision is hardly acceptable if it endangers the long-range health, if not the very existence, of the company. The dimensions of both present and future are to be considered in determining the critical balance between being too cautious and being too rash. While Drucker thought that far more problems were caused by being too cautious—he said that managers could neither eliminate nor avoid all risk—acting too quickly is a real and ever-present danger.

Example: Doing the Right Thing at the Wrong Time

You can do the right thing and still go awry if you introduce it at the wrong time. A few years ago, the New Jersey School Boards Association published the following regarding the expansion of K–8 education in the state:

> Imagine you are either the governor or commissioner of education of a highly diverse northeastern state. Like most states, yours is saddled with the "achievement gap" and students who lag behind their peers academically. Then imagine you are offered a solution that academics, legislators, educators, and parents agree may hold the key to closing the "achievement gap." Not only do you have all parties telling you that this is a success, but you actually have some proof that it works in the districts where it has been implemented. Wouldn't you jump at the opportunity to implement such a solution if you were governor or education commissioner? This is the type of program that makes history

books and creates a positive legacy of your tenure. Now imagine that you commit to this program publicly.

Finally, imagine you find out that your state is broke and probably cannot afford to pay for this worthwhile legacy-making program. What do you do? That is the situation that Gov. Jon Corzine and Commissioner Lucille Davy find themselves in. They are like children who have received no presents on Christmas, and have their face pressed up against the window of FAO Schwartz [sic]. So close . . . yet so far away.[4]

Corzine pressed forward anyway, and though today New Jersey's pre–K education system passed and is considered positively, the general impression of spending during New Jersey's economic challenges helped to defeat Corzine and put Governor Chris Christie into office.

Other industries are immune. Even the movie industry screws up the timing, sometimes with great regularity. MGM released *The Wizard of Oz* in 1939, with Judy Garland in the starring role when negotiations with the hugely popular Shirley Temple failed to pan out. However, the film with Garland in the role was well executed and won screen awards, and the timing was right. *The Wizard* was a box-office success and has since become a film classic. In 1940, seeking to duplicate this success, competitor 20th Century Fox got Shirley Temple for a similar fantasy based on a children's fairy tale called *The Bluebird*. How could it fail? But by then *The Wizard* had taken the market. Moreover, World War II was in full swing, and people's minds were on other things. It didn't help that *The Bluebird* was based on a German folktale. The film bombed (no pun intended). The fairy tale concept with Shirley Temple was right. The timing was not.

Four Specific Timing Decisions

There are four important aspects to consider in regard to good timing and strategy. These are:

1. When to take a specific action

2. The sequence of the actions to be taken

3. Whether the actions taken are continuous or discrete functions

4. Whether the actions are to be repeated

Knowing when to take each action is the basic timing decision. Consider the introduction of a new technology. You may think that if you develop something new, you should rush to introduce it. But this is rarely the case. If your company is known for being first with cutting-edge technology, that may be your competitive advantage. If having this advantage is important in your industry, and you have the resources to support it and can take the risk involved, by all means introduce the technology as soon as you develop it. In this case, it makes sense to invest the resources necessary to ensure that you are the very first with the innovation and are responsible for introducing it into the marketplace.

However, if you haven't got the resources that will guarantee an immediate impact, maybe it's better to let someone else get in there first and make the mistakes so that you can learn from them. Then you can introduce your more advanced or perfected product with less risk and a lower resource commitment.

The fact is a leading-edge technology company can miss the boat and still come out ahead. IBM was the technology leader in computers when someone at IBM did the flawed market research that concluded development of a personal computer would yield a mere 1,000 customers a year. Of course, this was utter nonsense, which Steve Jobs proved in founding Apple and creating an industry in the process. However, as we all know, IBM finally did enter the market, with a technologically inferior product, and took over the field by capitalizing on the weaknesses in Apple's strict control over software for its hardware. Actually, IBM wasn't just late to market; it was very late, with a host of other companies getting to market first.

This doesn't mean that being late is always the thing to do, of course. It does, however, show that for industries in which the state of technology is not the big differentiator, hanging back may have advantages. First entry into the marketplace has both advantages and disadvantages; it's up to you to think through the timing and weigh the options.

A manager must conclude, as Drucker did, that it's not enough to do the right thing. The successful decision maker must do the *right* thing at the *right* time.

CHAPTER TWENTY

How to Be a Managerial Fortune-Teller

"The best way to predict the future is to create it." That's Peter Drucker speaking. In fact, this has become one of Drucker's famous utterances. It has not only been quoted but also embossed on paperweights, developed for display on corporate walls, and printed in materials circulated around the world. In Beijing, I even saw some Chinese writing with Drucker's picture. A Chinese friend translated the text for me: "The best way to predict the future is to create it." At the California Institute of Advanced Management (CIAM), we modified it slightly and translated our version into Latin to make it our university credo: *Tantum vos can partum posterus*. Or, as we like to say in English, "Only you can create the future."

Drucker the Swami

Despite the fame of his proactive assertion, Drucker became a pretty good fortune-teller, which he implied was a second-best method for creating the future itself. When asked about his ability to predict the future so accurately, Drucker answered that he simply "looked through the window" and reported what he saw. Of course, he was fond of answering questions somewhat tongue-in-cheek. It's not that his answers weren't truthful, or that he was constantly making jokes, but it was easy to see why he was known as "that happy-go-lucky Austrian." At least that's how his mother-in-law described him, as told by his wife, Doris, in her book *Invent Radium or I'll Pull Your Hair.*[1]

The Only Person Drucker Listened to Besides His Wife

Once in class, when asked about his reputation for forecasting the future accurately, he answered, "I listen." After a dramatic pause, he added, "to myself." Drucker was neither arrogant nor excessively immodest, so he went on to explain; he said that you have to go one step further and ask yourself what the things you've seen or heard mean for the future. Stated another way, managers need to observe what is going on, and then take the additional step of analyzing this information and then deciding what will happen as a result of this event.

Drucker's Failure at Prediction

To my knowledge, Peter Drucker failed at his own method of prediction only once, and that was by not following his own advice. Or maybe he hadn't yet developed his methodology. However, you can't speak about his spectacular success as a management guru and fortune-teller without noting his first big public prediction, which was a bust. Moreover, and unfortunately for him, this prediction was widely disseminated. In a newspaper column published shortly before the 1929 stock market crash, Drucker predicted a rosy future and a bull market. He had to eat humble pie a few weeks later, in an article he wrote about the market crash, published in the *Frankfurter General-Anzeiger* and titled "Panic on the New York Stock Exchange."

As he told us in class, had he "looked through the window" and drawn some simple conclusions from the unsupported financial bubble that was brewing, he could hardly have made this mistake. Writing that article must have been difficult for him. It was the last time he made any predictions about the stock market, though his confidence in his ability to listen to himself and develop his methodology never flagged.

The Wisdom of Drucker's Prediction Methodology

Analysis of internal corporate information, such as cash flow, liquidity, productivity, competency, resource allocation information, and so on, by itself is useful only for short-term tactics. Drucker knew that a strategy of any sort had to be based on information about "markets, customers and noncustomers; about technology in one's own industry and others; about worldwide finance; and about the changing world economy."[2]

It doesn't matter whether the future you want to create is internal or external to your company. You begin by focusing your attention on what's going on in your area of interest. There are a vast number of items that will interest you, and they are constantly changing. Even trends are important, but sometimes changes can occur very rapidly. For example, the ubiquitous slide rule, carried for years by every practicing engineer for mathematical calculations, began to vanish within a year of the introduction of the handheld electronic calculator. That development should have caused leaders in many organizations to think through what this would mean for future operations: for engineers who would be able to make calculations more quickly and accurately; for companies producing slide rules; for planners who could anticipate jobs getting done with fewer errors, reworks, and costs; and many other ramifications. For example, HR people could also plan for a reduced need for engineers and others working with slide rules, in the same way that computers and answering machines resulted in a reduced need for secretaries.

Research Please, and Watch Your Assumptions

Looking through the window frequently requires research. This research may be primary or secondary; primary research entails interviews, business surveys, and a personal quest for the answers. Secondary research involves consulting other sources, including the library, the Internet, and previous studies conducted by your company, within the industry, or by the government. Secondary research is generally done first because it is already available. Do that first, before you spend the time and money to do primary research.

However, collecting this information is only part of the challenge. In fact, Drucker said that if you stop after just doing the research, you are heading for trouble. IBM made a major mistake when it considered developing a personal computer. This was a big computer company, and it built big mainframe computers. (Think of computers the size of a room—that's what IBM researchers had in mind.) As a result, IBM's market research told them that the market for personal computers was limited to about 1,000 customers—if they were lucky. I mentioned this in the previous chapter, but it's worth repeating because this kind of faulty reaction is almost inevitable when a product doesn't yet exist. It is difficult for consumers or businesses to feel comfortable about shelling out hundreds of dollars for a product that no one has seen or used yet.

What's the answer? Drucker suggested that leaders look at the market—through the window—when the product, service, or idea doesn't yet exist. His advice was to avoid making assumptions about such attributes as potential size, as this invariably leads you astray.

The Future Is a Result of the Past

What is going to happen in the future as a result of what has already happened in the past? That is the important part of the analysis equation. Joe Cossman, the man who sold more than a million "ant farms" for children and other unusual products, said that when you have a strong interest in a particular subject, you needn't worry about finding new products because everything you see ("through the window") is in some way associated with your passion.

Cossman was always looking for new products he could promote. He looked through the window and found that his strong interest in finding new products made his observations self-focusing—no matter which "window" he looked out. Once, he bought 40,000 pieces of junk jewelry on a short chain for less than a penny each. Why would anyone want to pay $400 for 40,000 pieces of anything that could have no possible use? The jewelry sat in Cossman's storeroom for some months.

Then a hypnotist claimed he had caused a subject to regress into a past life while entranced. This was Bridey Murphy, who became an international sensation. And suddenly there was a lot of interest in hypnotism. In order to understand what it was all about, Joe enrolled in a course. The instructor told him that, to induce a trance, he needed a point of fixation. "I've got 40,000 points of fixation," Joe told his instructor. He hired the instructor. Together, they designed a short course and made a recording on how to induce a hypnotic trance—using one of his jewelry pieces on a chain, which Cossman now described as a "trance inducer." The whole package, including one piece of jewelry, sold for about $5. That was a pretty hefty markup. Cossman had looked through the window and saw that tremendous interest in Bridey Murphy and interest in hypnotism would lead to a demand for ways to practice this phenomenon.

Change Is Inevitable—What Are You Going to Do About It?

We know that change is inevitable. But change is *caused* by events that have already occurred. Drucker suggested that all we need to do is look at events that have already taken place and decide what will happen as a result.

When foreign-made automobiles first hit the American market, it was Volkswagen that American car companies were concerned about, not the Japanese models. In response, Ford introduced the Falcon, Plymouth had the Valiant, and Chevrolet had the Corvair. However, Americans wanted more on their vehicles than what the bare-bones

Volkswagen provided in those days, and so the smaller American cars grew in size in a few short years, until they were simply scaled-down versions of the full-size American cars. Sales slowly eroded for all three models, and so all three were withdrawn from the market. These cars offered essentially the same options, so all three automobile manufacturers looked through the window and saw the same thing.

One car manufacturer, however, took another look and noticed that demand for *certain* features was increasing even as sales for its vehicles were declining. These features were bucket seats, "four-on-the-floor" gearshifts, and padded dashboards. Only Ford asked itself what this meant. It realized there was increasing demand for a sports-touring type of vehicle. The Mustang was kept under strict wraps until it was released. When eventually introduced, the Mustang generated tremendous sales to fulfill this new demand—which had been easily predicted by "looking through the window" and analyzing events that had already taken place and what they meant for the future.

Cossman's hypnotism package and the Ford Mustang are both marketing examples. But the same principle applies to everything else in management or business. Something significant happens. What is likely to occur as a result? What does it mean in your work? How can you use this to create a desired, or at least a more desirable future?

In summary, here are Drucker's thoughts about the information a leader needs to create the future:

- Look through the window and examine your environment.

- Consider both the general and the specific questions relating to your organization.

- Decide what is likely to happen as a result of significant events that have already occurred.

- Consider these factors as you develop a plan and take action to create the future you want for yourself or your organization.

CHAPTER TWENTY-ONE

What Are You Going to Do About It?

Years ago, Peter Drucker was giving one of his all-day seminars. I think it was called "A Day with Drucker." During the Q&A period, a clearly distressed individual launched into a long monologue about the challenges he faced in his company. These challenges appeared insurmountable. It was obvious that he expected Drucker to solve his problems, telling him what to do. At first, Peter listened politely. Finally, as the man went on and on, Drucker interrupted. "Okay," said Peter, "so you are in trouble. What are you going to do about it?"

We Need to Take Responsibility

Early in what has been labeled the Great Recession, the CEOs of the three largest U.S. automobile companies flew to Washington, D.C., in their private jets to testify before Congress and ask for a multibillion-dollar bailout. Their argument was that these hard economic times weren't their fault, and unless Congress helped out, a lot of people would lose their jobs. They didn't ask what to do about it because they knew: "Give us money."

The talk of a bailout for the automotive industry was already controversial. The day before, the *Los Angeles Times* reported that one senator said something like: "Look, I've heard from my constituents. They are very much against this. One works for a foreign automobile company which manufactures cars in the United States. He told me that he makes $40 an hour. He also informed me that the average worker salary at the 'Big Three' is almost twice that. He wanted to know why we should use his money so that some guy can make twice what he does for doing the same job. This worker is right. These people are in trouble due to the mismanagement of their companies. All companies are hurt when people aren't buying their products. These companies are in trouble too, and must take action to do whatever they need to get profitable given these economic conditions which we all face."

The senator was correct in his assessment of the situation. How much people should be paid is really just a symptom of a greater problem. We cannot control nature, and we can't control most aspects of the business or economic environment. We can't control technological advances, and we can't control the changing beliefs or preferences of society. Regardless, as managers and leaders we are responsible for the welfare of our employees and the performance of our organizations, be they small units or giant companies.

I think Peter Drucker would have responded to the pleas of the automotive CEOs with this question: "What are you going to do about it?"

Example: Business as Usual

Someone pointed out that each of these CEOs, coming from the same city, had flown to Washington, D.C., in individual corporate jets that cost each company about $20,000. The CEOs didn't consider flying commercial, much less economy class. They didn't even consider flying together on a single airplane. Many companies have corporate jets. Normally they can save time and money by getting the executive where he needs to be quickly and efficiently, thereby helping him do a better job. But these CEOs were asking the government for a $56 billion bailout. As one congressman said, "Somebody said they're handing out free money in Washington, and these three came to get it."

Their trip to Washington was a clear signal that these leaders envisioned only "business as usual." As they saw it, the economic situation wasn't their fault, so somebody else should pick up the tab. They'd be perfectly happy to make some minor changes in the production of their vehicles, but they would press on doing everything just as always—at taxpayer expense, of course. And when that money ran out, they could return for more money from Uncle Sam.

No, Drucker would have told the three: "Okay, so you are in trouble. Sure it's the economy. You can't change that. But what are *you* going to do about it?"

My point is not whether the three executives should have been given the money, which they eventually received. The second time they came to Washington, they had the good sense to drive there, if only for appearance's sake. But many people wondered whether they had really learned their lesson. Today, the three companies are all profitable again, and I'm certain the executives are all smiles.

Example: Those That Were Too Big to Fail

It wasn't long before these automobile companies and other organizations, especially in the financial industry, which had been termed "too big to fail," were profitable once again. Some were making more money than ever before. One financial institution that received government assistance turned right around and rewarded its senior executives large bonuses. But this is not a new story. Years earlier, Drucker had pointed out the unconscionable anomaly of executives' huge compensation packages while they laid off thousands of employees. Talk about fiddling while Rome burns!

No wonder Drucker warned so emphatically that this meltdown would happen. He said that the gluttony of both outlandish executive salaries and the continually escalating demands of unions would eventually demand a terrible price.[1] Many in both camps were angry at him for saying this, but he was right.

Got Problems? What Are You Going to Do About It?

So here we are. Now what do we do? Drucker's main point is that we are ourselves responsible and cannot rely on someone else to give us the magic potion that will cause all the bad things to go away. However, there are general Drucker principles that can guide us in what we do. Here are a few:

- *Take charge and decide what you are going to do next.* Don't focus on what has happened or expect some miracle to put everything right. No matter how much you wish, you can't wish the problem away. So accept it and move on. This is true whether you are the CEO in charge, a manager who is trying to hold his or her unit together, or someone who has just been laid off.

A billionaire I know is a foreign national. While he was visiting in the United States some years ago, someone in his government launched an investigation of his operations, based on hearsay. It greatly limited his operations, he lost the first of hundreds of thousands of dollars, and his business empire came under government pressure and scrutiny. There was no warrant for his arrest, but he knew that if he returned home he might well be arrested and be able to accomplish very little.

So he put his company's day-to-day operations in the hands of a trusted subordinate and he worked through his lawyers to take many actions that were needed. He didn't waste time feeling sorry for himself or asking why this was happening to him. He stayed away while he made the decisions that kept his businesses in operation, working simultaneously to clear his name. It took months, but ultimately he was successful and things returned to normal. In fact, his businesses are fully recovered, bigger and more successful than ever. The lesson here is that when bad things happen, you don't sit around waiting for a miracle and feeling sorry for yourself.

- *Use your resources and don't get discouraged.* Even under the worst conditions, you have resources, advantages, and strengths that you may not have considered. Write these down. No matter who you are or what your situation, others have been there before and have overcome their problems. Do a little searching on the Internet and find out how they did it. Others have done "the impossible." So can you.

It doesn't matter whether you are a Republican or Democrat, or whether you support President Obama and his policies or not. No one can deny what he accomplished in his campaign for election in 2008 and the huge challenges he had to overcome. Even within his own party, no one thought that he had a chance. Limited government experience—in fact, limited experience of any kind. He was best known for the highly acclaimed keynote speech he had written and delivered at the 2004 Democratic Convention in Boston. Do you remember Hillary Clinton's challenge to Obama four years later? "What is he going to do if he gets a crisis call in the middle of the night? Say that he has this great speech?" One well-known African-American politician told me: "Obama has a lot of ability and charisma. He'll be president one day, but not this year—this is Hillary's year."

Obama's election proved that we all have personal resources to overcome a situation, even if the experts say we can't do it. If you or your company is in an impossible situation, what are your resources? I don't know. You are in trouble: What are you going to do about it?

- *Develop a plan.* Decide where you want to go and work out detailed short- and long-range plans to get there from where you are.

Tony Robbins was dead broke and living in an apartment that didn't even have a kitchen. It had a bathtub, though, and that's where Robbins washed his dishes. Robbins had no college degree, was barely out of his teens, and there was no one who could support him while he struggled to stay alive. Then he lost his job. He took charge and considered his resources. He decided what he was going to do, and he wrote down a plan for how he was going to get there. It didn't take long until he became both wealthy and famous as the preeminent motivational speaker in the world, consulted by kings and heads of state worldwide.

- *Work your plan.* Nothing happens until you take action, so do it! The ancient Chinese seer Lao-tzu said that a journey of a thousand miles begins with the first step. Take that first step.

As Mary Kay Ash did when her husband died suddenly two weeks prior to opening her cosmetics company, she got her saleswomen together, told them how they were going to implement her plan, and they went out and helped Mary Kay grow a billion-dollar company.

* * *

I'm told that more people became millionaires during the Great Depression than ever before. This is true, but it is misleading. Most people in this category became millionaires because of the demand for goods and services that came with the onset of World War II. However, offsetting those companies helped by the war, there still were many that not only survived but also prospered during the Great Depression. Smart companies like Procter & Gamble increased their advertising and took advantage of a new medium—radio—much as Barack Obama took advantage of the Internet, cell phones, and YouTube during the 2008 presidential election.

However bad any situation looks, Drucker advised, extraordinary leaders are successful because they do things that ordinary leaders just won't do. Are you and your company in trouble? What are you going to do about it?

PART THREE

Marketing and Innovation

CHAPTER TWENTY-TWO

Can Marketing and Selling Be Adversarial?

Pick up any marketing textbook, and you'll find "tactical marketing variables" described variously, either using that name or described as "strategic marketing variables," "the controllable factors," "the marketing mix," "the 4 Ps," and the like. Let's go with the 4 Ps.

The 4 Ps is a term proposed by Professor E. Jerome McCarthy, of Michigan State University, based on his categorization of marketing issues and disseminated worldwide through his book *Basic Marketing*. As Jerry McCarthy told me more than thirty years ago, prior to his creation of this categorization there were so many different known marketing factors, all completely unorganized, that one didn't know how to proceed.[1] McCarthy named these four main factors Product, Price, Promotion, and Place. Product and Price are self-explanatory; Place has to do with physical distribution and distribution structure. However, it's Promotion that has buried within itself what we call "selling."

Marketing encompasses all of these variables because, while each is tactical, marketing is strategic. So the 4 Ps and their subsets all support marketing. Now you'll be able to see the monumental problem that Drucker created when he asserted that there was an unusual relationship between marketing and selling.

"Marketing and selling are not complementary and may be adversarial." This is one of his most astonishing statements and I imagine many marketing professors might have been ready to take him on about it. Yet, although I certainly had my doubts when I first heard him say it, he was right. Selling may be a subset of marketing, but it can still be adversarial to marketing because marketing is strategic and selling is tactical.

Example: "My Son, the Musician"

Some years ago, my old friend and wizard marketer Joe Cossman (the man who created the "ant farm" described in Chapter 31 and sold more than a million of them to children worldwide) was telling me about the time he had such high sales that it almost put him out of business. With sudden insight upon hearing his story, I finally grasped what Drucker had meant.

Cossman had gotten control of an unusual product, called "My Son, the Musician." The inventor told Cossman that it was guaranteed to end parental problems in training very young children to use the toilet bowl properly. The device consisted of a plastic bowl with a sensing device embedded in the inside that connected to a music box on the outside. When the bowl sensed liquid, it would immediately begin to play a popular nursery tune.

Cossman wrote the advertising copy and rushed "My Son, the Musician" into production. He engaged salespeople and began to promote the product through direct mail and through distributors. The potty trainer was well received; in fact, the number of items ordered through retailers prior to actual production was one of the highest of any of Cossman's many products. He thought he had hit the jackpot!

His enthusiasm ended when a child psychologist called to tell him that he was looking at future legal problems. "My Son, the Musician" worked all right. The problem was that it worked too well. It would absolutely potty-train the child; the problem was that using the potty would become permanently associated with music, not with the device. It doesn't take much imagination to grasp the consequences: Years later, that potty-trained youngster would grow up and urinate whenever he heard that music.

Cossman's distributors and salesmen had done a wonderful job, but if Cossman had continued to allow these spectacular sales, the lawsuits from former users would have put him out of business years later. The more product he sold, the greater the danger. So, sometimes high sales are adversarial to overall marketing strategy. Cossman may have found a way around this problem, but instead he chose to withdraw the product from the market.

Strategy Is More Important Than Tactics

Marketing strategy is employed at a higher level and is more important than selling tactics. Cossman's strategy was based on a flawed concept—flawed not because the idea was bad in itself but because of its unintended consequences. Robert E. Wood, who was chief executive officer of Sears, Roebuck, and Company during its years of greatest growth (and also a retired Army general with combat experience from WWI), stated: "Business is like war in one respect—if its grand strategy is correct, any number of tactical errors can be made, and yet the enterprise proves successful."[2] Unfortunately, the reverse is not true: One cannot overcome strategic errors by correct tactical implementation. If the strategy is wrong, competent tactical operations can only temporarily conceal the strategic blunder. And the wrongful employment of good tactical resources is a waste.

Good Selling Cannot Overcome Poor Marketing

Without sales there is no business, and thus the importance of sales is undeniable. That is why some people have the simplistic notion that effective selling automatically overcomes poor marketing strategy.

I recall some years ago that a professor at one of our leading universities expressed that idea in a journal article. He wrote that if the selling is good enough, it can overcome a bad strategy and result in high sales. However, this is misleading. The initial high sales may conceal a major problem that could result in disaster (as was the case with Cossman's potty product). Or it could cause the marketer to misallocate resources to a strategy that is far less efficient in creating customers or else allocate them to a business that should never have been entered in the first place.

Drucker wrote, "First decide what business you are in." And then he went on to say that the purpose of any business is to create a customer. This was Drucker's rationale for stating that marketing is the distinguishing basic function of business. In this sense, strategy or marketing is the means to create a customer. But strategy and tactics are not the same thing. A marketer whose strategy is actually a tactic is at great risk. Should that tactic fail, he will soon find himself in trouble. This is what happened to the company that has become a poster child for wrong government investment.

Example: A Strategic Misstep Embarrasses the U.S. Government

In 2005, a company called Solyndra was founded to design, manufacture, and sell solar photovoltaic (PV) systems—you know, solar cells. However, Solyndra's solar cells were not the conventional flat solar panels we sometimes see. Instead, they were cylindrical. Solyndra claimed that because of their unusual shape, these panels could capture more solar power than conventional panels, and they could do so without moving one millimeter. Also, because they could cover more of the typically available roof area, they produced more electricity on each rooftop where they were used.

The company was attractive to many, including the U.S. government, for a number of other reasons as well. First, there was the environmentally friendly aspect of the electricity produced. Then there was the hiring of over 1,000 employees at a time when jobs were beginning to get scarce. However, the strategy was a tactic: low pricing due to the materials used, design, and the new design. Of course, materials technology didn't stand still during this period. As a result, the formerly higher price of regular solar panels came down significantly as solar energy caught on and more conventional solar panels were produced and sold. Solyndra's panels became far more expensive than the traditional flat panels, and the total system became more expensive as well. Solyndra panels were still novel and technically more elegant and sophisticated, but there was no competitive advantage and hence the company failed.[3]

Solyndra's marketing was a *tactic* based on price. A closer look would have exposed the company's vulnerability. If the price of the standard solar panel came down—a virtual certainty as worldwide sales increased—it should have been obvious that Solyndra could not succeed despite its appearance of technological superiority.

Tactics Must Be Determined by Strategy

A marketer must first have a strategy firmly in mind. Then, he is in a position to develop the tactics to support that strategy. During the Great Depression, Procter & Gamble's president, Richard Deupree, realized that consumers were still buying essential household products. Moreover, the competitors were cutting back on their advertising. So, his strategy was to introduce a host of new, innovative products and to significantly increase advertising as competitors reduced theirs. This was a strategy he initiated in the face of significant pressure from P&G associates. But, at a time when his shareholders were demanding that he cut advertising budgets and reduce other expenses to avoid losses, Deupree did the opposite—but he did even more.

Just as candidate Barack Obama took advantage of new technology in the 2008 election to get his messages out to millions of potential voters, P&G used the radio as its breakthrough vehicle of advertising. It didn't sink all its money into print advertising, as did competitors. In 1933, P&G began advertising Oxydol, a laundry soap it had acquired several years earlier. It sponsored a new radio show called "Ma Perkins." Like the reality TV shows of today, the first program was launched at some risk. But fortunately for P&G, it was a gamble that paid off. Soon the radio introduction for the show was expanded to "Oxydol's Own Ma Perkins." The sponsorship was so successful that only a few years later P&G was sponsoring twenty-one other radio shows, all associated with specific products. P&G not only significantly increased its sales and market share, it doubled its radio advertising budget every two years during the Depression, and it virtually built the daytime radio industry single-handedly. P&G's advertising and sponsorships even gave a new term to the English language, "the soap opera."[4,5,6]

Synergistic, Not Complementary

Selling and marketing may not be complementary, but tactics should be complementary as well as synergistic. *Synergistic* means that the whole should be greater than the sum of the individual parts or tactics. During the Great Depression, P&G emphasized product and advertising. Both worked together; Oxydol actually was better than competitive products at the time. It really did make clothes come out four or five times whiter. They tested it and it did save the poor housewife twenty-five minutes of pounding wet clothes against washing boards with some slight assistance from suds, as necessary with other brands.

Drucker was right again! A marketer needs to ensure that selling is complementary, synergistic, and not adversarial and that strategy is considered primary even with the most brilliant tactics. Moreover, a tactic cannot be allowed to become a strategy.

CHAPTER TWENTY-THREE

The Five Great Marketing Sins

Early on in his career, Peter Drucker declared that there are only two basic business functions: "The first is innovation, and the second is marketing." From 1975 to 1995, Drucker wrote a column for the *Wall Street Journal*. On October 21, 1993, his column was entitled "The Five Deadly Business Sins."[1] Confirming his assertion that marketing was one of the two basic business functions, all five sins had to do with marketing.

Drucker easily could have called them "The Five Deadly Marketing Sins." This column was pure Drucker: He warned against what many experts were advising and other "beliefs" that "everybody knew." And he hastened to demonstrate that their advice was false. According to Drucker, these are the five deadly sins:

1. Seeking high profit margins and premium pricing

2. Charging what the market will bear

3. Using cost-driven pricing

4. Focusing on past winners

5. Giving problems priority over opportunities

Let's take a look at each, but call them what Drucker really meant.

Seeking High Profit Margins and Premium Pricing

This sin is easily the most common of the five; however, it sounds like common sense. Why shouldn't marketers seek high profit margins? I remember early on being told in an MBA class in marketing that one concept of marketing a new product was to enter the marketplace with a high price and then, as the market matured and competitors joined the marketplace, use the high profits won earlier to fight off the competition—for example, with increased advertising or some other good use of that financial advantage.

Drucker thought this approach was extremely dangerous, and he illustrated his reservations by example. For instance, the fax machine. The strategy of the American inventor company, Xerox, was to keep the profits high by staying ahead of the competition with a "better" product. Sounds good—and right out of a marketing textbook.

Xerox continually added new features to justify increasing the price. Unfortunately, it was clear to sales prospects that many of these new features did little to add value and were largely unnecessary. At best, they contributed only marginally to the product's performance. Xerox might have at least made them optional, so that customers would have a choice. But they didn't. Their eyes were on keeping the margins and profits high, so they could later use that cash to fight off competitors, just as taught in B-School. Moreover, they failed to heed Drucker's cautionary note that it is not what the manufacturer values, but what the customer values that's important.

The strategy was wrong, proven by the fact that the Japanese took over the market, not just in the United States but also worldwide. The Japanese looked at this breakthrough product and did a little re-engineering. However, they recognized that the key to capturing the market was not advanced features and high price. When they got it right, they entered the market with a product that did the job well at a much lower and more reasonable price. The Japanese fax machines may not have had all of the bells and whistles, but they captured Xerox's market with great ease. We may still incorrectly ask an employee to "Xerox" a copy for us, but chances are the individual is "Xeroxing" on a Japanese-made fax machine, which today may be Korean or Chinese made.

While it may seem obvious and intuitive that wider margins should lead to higher profits, *total profit is margin multiplied by sales*. So what the marketer should be seeking is an optimum profit margin that, when combined with sales over time, will equal maximum profits. This still allows for the accumulation of profits with which to take on oncoming competitors, but it does so without creating a market for those competitors.

Drucker considered this sin the worst part of the whole business. He found that the strategy of high profit margins, combined with tactics of premium pricing, invariably creates a market for the competition and can result in loss of the entire market to a competitor.[2]

I would like to add a caveat here: Avoid simply and arbitrarily freezing an original price and always seeking a low price, blindly and forever. Henry Ford kept Model T pricing low and sold millions of cars, not even allowing deviation from his one color (black). Drucker even quoted Henry Ford: "We can sell the Model T at such a low price only because it earns such a nice profit."[3] However, Ford did this for too long. As prospects grew more willing to pay for options, even color variance, the Model T sales declined. Ford didn't lose his entire market, but his determination to focus on standardization and low price caused him to slip to number two in sales, behind General Motors, for forty years.

While this caveat doesn't alter Drucker's cautionary warning in the opposite direction, especially since he spoke of the *worship* of high margins and premium pricing, it does tell us that unlike diamonds, strategies are not forever.

Charging What the Market Will Bear

Let's say that you have a patent or a secret formula. Conventional wisdom says to charge as much as the market will pay. The rationale is the same as for the first sin. As your competition appears, you can use the extra cash you accumulated through charging the maximum to fight off any and all competitors that try to enter the marketplace. Or you can then lower your price below that of your competitors. This way, they can never catch you.

Many consider charging what the market will bear to be a guaranteed marketing strategy when entering the market before the competition and when you have some leverage to keep competitors away. But is it? It is similar to, but not the same as, seeking high margins and premium pricing. Here, you just keep increasing the price because you can—and the customer is willing to pay, or may need or want the product so badly that he feels he must pay it. But this is worse than premium pricing. At least the latter has a little finesse, and is supposedly involved with finding customer needs and filling them. But charging whatever the market will bear is a brutal strategy. It's damn the customers and full speed ahead!

The only sure thing about charging what the market will bear is that you will lose your market—and a lot sooner than you might think. A very high price creates an almost risk-free opportunity for your competitors to jump in and seize your market. All they need to do is fill the same need. Business risk is always present, so when a nearly risk-free opportunity presents itself, it is a wonderful incentive. Moreover, the higher your price, the lower is the competition's risk and the even greater incentive to jump in and compete.

When DuPont patented and introduced nylon, it sold it at a price that it anticipated it would keep selling it at for at least five years. What were these DuPont people—economic psychics? How could they know what price they would have to charge in five years to keep competitors in check? Easy. They had the history of previous products like nylon. They could estimate the improvement in manufacturing techniques, the buying in higher quantities, and other advantages of the economy of scale. They could also factor in mistakes they would no longer make as they gained experience and expertise. Boeing used the same techniques a few years later to estimate the cost of building thousands of B-17 bombers during World War II, even though they built only one prototype.

Drucker estimated that DuPont's price was less than half of the price it could have sold the product for successfully at the time. However, with this advanced pricing, DuPont had no difficulty keeping its competitors out of the market. In the process, DuPont made nylon affordable to millions of women and kept the competitors away for years.[4]

Using Cost-Driven Pricing

Cost-driven pricing means that you simply add up all your costs, and then add the desired profit, and there you are—the price you should charge. It's all very logical, but it is also simply wrong. (By the way, this is how the government insists contractors price the products that they buy. It's supposed to ensure both competition and a "fair" price. All you need to do is look at government cost overruns to see how well the cost-driven pricing approach is working, even when insisted upon by the customer.)

Drucker said that instead of cost-driven pricing, you needed to do price-driven *costing*. That is, you need to start at the other end with the right price, and then to work backward to determine your allowable costs. Drucker blamed the loss of the consumer-electronics industry and the machine-tool industry in the United States directly on this deadly sin. (One begins to understand why Drucker called these deadly sins, and not simply marketing mistakes.)

Focusing on Past Winners

Drucker actually called this "slaughtering tomorrow's opportunity on the altar of yesterday." He wanted to emphasize how managers commit this sin in the name of past successes. Drucker's label is more flamboyant, but mine is more succinct. After IBM recovered from its immense gaffe of missing the PC market (mentioned in Chapters 19 and 20), it still insisted on subordinating its newly won PC business to its old winner, the mainframe computer. Not only did resources go primarily to the mainframes, but the new IBM PC marketers were discouraged from selling their product to mainframe customers, lest those customers mistake what business IBM was really in. The net result was that IBM did not reap the fruits of its amazing recovery in taking leadership of the PC market away from Apple. Instead, its "achievement" was mostly in encouraging other newcomers to create IBM clones—and this major marketing blunder didn't help its mainframe business in any way.[5]

Giving Problems Priority over Opportunities

Drucker saw that many companies put their best-performing people to work solving old problems with businesses or products that were already on their way out. During WWII, many Allied aircraft companies spent their resources trying to make old reciprocal engine piston planes fly faster when they had just about reached their maximum. It wasn't that they didn't know about jet engines or rocket-engine technology, but they applied most of their resources to gaining relatively small advances in speed—in essence, doing the best they could with the tried-and-true. Meanwhile, the German aircraft industry forged ahead despite terrific environmental problems from Allied air superiority near the end of the war. As a result, Germany had both jet- and rocket-engine aircraft in combat before the Allies had done much but fly and experiment with prototypes.

Those committing this last marketing sin frequently assign new opportunities to those lacking experience or ability, and put their first team on solving old problems. This frequently occurs, as is the case with many things, because we let our egos get in the way. Otherwise smart marketers pour a lot of resources, money, and people into fending off someone's encroachment into one of their established markets. Sure, it may be declining, but this is their turf and they won't surrender it easily. So ego is involved in defending what may be barely worthwhile, while real opportunity is seized by a competitor.

* * *

When Peter Drucker claimed that these were sins, and not mere mistakes, he wasn't exaggerating. Sinners take heed!

CHAPTER TWENTY-FOUR

You Can't Get the Right Strategy from a Formula

About the time that I became a new professor, the university hired a large consulting firm to assess its course offerings and programs and to develop an overall strategy for fulfilling its mission and meeting the needs of the community. All professors, staff, and administrators were invited to a multihour presentation on the consultants' approach. That is, it was explained what they intended to do and the process they would use to recommend the programs and courses that should be maintained, name the ones that should be dropped, and suggest the new programs that should be initiated to achieve the most efficient results, given the level of resources we had to work with.

The consultant team was articulate, well dressed, and polished. They walked us through a well-constructed presentation, showing us how they had developed their strategy formula. It was a variation of portfolio management with the familiar four-celled matrix (shooting stars, cash cows, question marks, and dogs) developed by the Boston Consulting Company, as modified by the more complex nine-celled matrix developed by the McKinsey Company for General Electric some years later. They took pains to explain their quantitative analysis, which would result in explicit directions as to when, where, and how much money we should invest. It was an impressive presentation that resulted in a strategy well supported by complex equations and research. If nothing else, the study was notable for the huge amount of money it had cost. It was implemented exactly as directed and it failed miserably.

The Drucker Approach Was Different

Drucker's views on *strategy* were quite different from those taught by many others. He did not believe in "portfolio management" or quantitative equations for strategy development, although he accepted that a thorough analysis was required and that figures were an important input, useful in helping to arrive at strategy decisions. However, he felt that every situation had to be approached individually, with common sense based on history.

This approach is probably one reason that Drucker, although a self-proclaimed "nonhistorian," used historical examples—not always business examples—to illustrate his concepts. And though the word *strategy* comes from the Greek word *strategos*, which means "the art of the general," he did not believe that "business is war"—although he had an impressive knowledge of military strategy, which he thoroughly enjoyed discussing.

Even though he did not view marketing or business as warfare, Drucker recognized that there were certain principles of strategy for any organization—or any other purpose—that parallel military strategy. Both the military and your typical organization operate on a "theory of business." But Drucker used that strategy to convert the theory of business into performance—that the purpose of strategy was to enable an organization to achieve its desired results in an unpredictable environment.

The Drucker Way

In practice, Peter Drucker first looked at a company's overall objectives, and whether they matched what the business of the company was, what the business should be, who the customer was, what the customer wanted, and, most importantly, what the customer valued in fulfilling his or her wants and needs. He then developed strategy, looking at the relevant events that had occurred and determining what they would mean for the future. He called the results of this analysis "certainties." Pleasant or unpleasant, the "certainties" had to be faced squarely. In other words, he started with an analysis of the marketplace, then sought to identify the relevant events that would result in future certainties.

Drucker knew that risk could not be avoided. In fact, he believed that some risk was a requirement for success. The future was always unknown, and unknowns always mean risk. If there were little or no risk, this would instead mean that the corporation was not aiming high enough. According to Drucker, the risks from unknowns could best be dealt with by taking the initiative to create one's own future. Therefore, in developing strategy, a manager has to plan the actions that will achieve the goals he or she has established. Of course, major threats have to be identified, along with alternative courses of action should these threats become realities.

Four Questions That Must Be Answered

Any company's strategy has to incorporate the answers to four Drucker questions:

1. What opportunities does the company want to pursue and what risks is it willing and able to accept in this pursuit?

2. What is the scope and structure of the organization's strategy, including the right balance among such aspects as specialization, diversification, and integration?

3. What are the acceptable trade-offs between time and money, and between in-house execution and using a merger, acquisition, joint venture, or some other external means of achieving the company's objectives and attaining its goals?

4. What organizational structure is appropriate to the company's economic realities, its opportunities, and its performance expectations?

A recognition that strategy has to be based on these four questions led to a methodology that Drucker adopted, which was more inferred than spelled out as a "by the numbers" process. It follows various approaches to strategy that probably began with the Boston Consulting Group's four-celled matrix (also discussed in Chapter 30) and recognition of a relationship between market share and market growth.

Ten Principles of Strategy Development

Drucker integrated goals and objectives (what the business should be) with the variables of the situation and the resources needed, and added his judgment based on his own observations. The latter, of course, was the most difficult to grasp. I knew his judgment involved certain principles, so based on my knowledge and research into strategy, I came up with the following principles that a strategist should consider:[1]

1. *Make a full commitment to a defined objective.* Drucker made it clear that the defined objective was what the business should be. This is why he granted so much importance to analyzing this issue. The objective must be precisely defined, and then the corporation must be fully committed to achieving it.

2. *Seize the initiative and keep it until you succeed.* There are many examples of individuals or organizations that have had a great idea,

but then delayed in developing that idea or bringing it to market. Or, in some instances, someone ceased work at the very point of achieving success. The Wright brothers were the first to achieve actual success in powered flight. But did you know that in 1891, twelve years before the Wrights flew, an astronomer named Samuel Langley built a model of a plane that he called an Aerodrome, which included a steam-powered engine?

Langley's model flew for almost a mile before it ran out of fuel. As a result of his success, he received a $50,000 grant to build a full-size Aerodrome (that equates to about $1,250,000 today). However, his full-size airplane crashed and Langley was so disappointed that he gave up trying. But here's the interesting part. Flyer Glenn Curtis modified Langley's Aerodrome in 1914 and made several successful flights with it. Had Langley persisted, it would have been he, and not the Wrights, who first demonstrated manned flight.[2]

This principle says you must get the initiative and keep it until you achieve your goal. Drucker emphasized not theory, or even planning, but action.

3. *Economize to mass your resources.* You can't be strong everywhere, because your resources will always be limited. The idea is to economize where your efforts and resources are not critical and to concentrate them where they are needed most. Essentially, you must concentrate your superior resources at the decisive point in any situation.

This is exactly what Drucker was saying when he asked Jack Welch of General Electric his two famous questions: "If you weren't already in a business, would you enter it today?" and "If the answer is no, what are you going to do about it?"

4. *Use strategic positioning.* To achieve any strategic objective, you need to make changes and adapt, owing to environmental or other unexpected factors. Hence, you may need to modify your ap-

proach and your positioning in the marketplace, even as you continue to work toward your objective. That translates to this: If what you are doing isn't working, you need to adjust your strategy. It's true that persistence is an immensely valuable trait for reaching any goal; however, maintaining a faulty strategy in pursuit of a worthwhile goal is foolish—or worse.

5. *Do the unexpected.* When you have competition, surprise your competition by doing the unexpected. This principle can also be profitably applied to customers, so long as the surprise is a pleasant one. For example, giving your customers, or those you service in an organization, more than they expect is almost always a valuable surprise.

6. *Keep things simple.* Someone at NASA once calculated that if every one of the parts in just one of its rockets was 99.9 percent reliable, the rocket would fail 50 percent of the time. We would have had to curtail our space program in short order. That is, the more things that can go wrong, the more will go wrong. If you want less to go wrong, keep your strategy simple.

7. *Prepare multiple simultaneous alternatives.* Since some actions inspired by your thinking are going to fail, always have an alternative action that can secure an alternative objective. This alternative action should already be thought out and ready to be implemented.

8. *Take the indirect route to your objective.* Moving directly against any human thought or endeavor always arouses opposition—people hold on all the more strongly to their present thinking. In truth, no one likes to be sold anything, whether it's a product or an idea. However, most people are eager to take advantage of a bargain or adopt an idea that will benefit them. The difference is subtle, but the results can be decisive.

Remember, the direct route will always lead to the strongest opposition. The same principle holds true in facing the competition.

Avoid the position where your competition is strongest, and make your approach where it is the weakest. (This concept was first developed and analyzed by B. H. Liddell Hart—probably the greatest military strategist and, some would say, simply the greatest strategist of the last century.)

9. *Practice timing and sequencing.* The Bible says that there is a time for every purpose under heaven. The reverse is true, too. Implementing the "right" strategy at the wrong time or in the wrong sequence can be just as ineffective as if it were all wrong. You've heard the saying, "He was ahead of his time." Yet, someone with the same idea at the right time may be extraordinarily successful. Bottled water is very successful today, and some branded names command very high prices. Yet some years ago, the idea of anyone's paying for bottled water, unless it was from Lourdes, would have been considered a joke.

10. *Exploit your success.* Don't stop or slow down when you achieve your objectives. If you don't stay continually *ahead* of your competition, you are simply giving the competition another chance to stop you.

* * *

In summary, to develop strategy, decide on your objectives; find the "certainties" in the situation; bring together the certainties, the resources required, and the variables; decide on the action steps to implement the strategy; and take action.

CHAPTER TWENTY-FIVE

Drucker's Four Approaches to Entrepreneurial Marketing

Years ago, Peter Drucker wrote a book on entrepreneurship. I was not surprised at the timing because it was 1985, and entrepreneurship was all the rage. I had even written several books on the subject myself. What did surprise me was Drucker's writing a book on that subject. I had never known him to be interested in entrepreneurship. However, there were lots of things that I hadn't learned about Peter Drucker, even after my doctoral work with him and our becoming friends afterwards.

But I shouldn't have been surprised, because Peter Drucker knew a lot about a lot of subjects. I soon found out that he had taught entrepreneurship in New York in the 1950s. His book *Innovation and Entrepreneurship* is fascinating, and I recommend it to anyone interested in the subject.[1] Some months later, I wrote a review of the book for a business publication.[2]

Peter Drucker, Entrepreneur

Drucker was himself an entrepreneur, and in many ways, in every way, he promoted entrepreneurial approaches for all business functions, entrepreneurial or not. Most well known is his suggestion that any manager ask himself "What business are you in?" This question applies to both entrepreneurial and nonentrepreneurial activities, to all specialties, and even to the most junior-level employees as well as the CEOs.

Equally applicable to all situations are Drucker's entrepreneurial ideas about success in business. He named four general approaches for success in entrepreneurship, each having its own prerequisites and its best fit for certain situations:

1. Achieving dominance

2. Supplying the missing ingredient

3. Finding and occupying an "ecological niche"

4. Changing economic characteristics

Let's take a look at each of these.

Achieving Dominance

Drucker gave this approach the rather imaginative title of "Fastest with the Mostest," a phrase he attributed to a Confederate cavalry general during the Civil War. The general was Nathan Bedford Forrest, one of the wealthiest men in the South at the start of the war. Unfortunately, Forrest's wealth came mostly from the slave trade. He rejected a commission in the new Confederate Army and enlisted as a private. Yet he finished the war as one of the Confederacy's most successful generals. Forrest had mastered the secret of concentrating his force at a decisive position to achieve superior combat power before his adversary could do so, and thus his men dominated the battlefield. Let's translate this into business terms.

Example: Howard Schultz and Starbucks

Starbucks opened in Seattle, Washington, in 1971, with a single outlet selling one product, roasted coffee that someone else had brewed. Fifteen years later, in 1986, the company had grown to six stores. The following year, the founders sold out to former Starbucks employee Howard Schultz. Only two years afterwards, Schultz had expanded to forty-six stores; and three years after that, he went to 140 stores. By 1994, the number had doubled to 280. Schultz clearly knew how to dominate a market, and he did so.

Like any business, Starbucks has had its ups and downs since Schultz took ownership. But no one can deny his successful strategy of being "the fustest with the mostest." Today, Starbucks is the largest coffeehouse company in the world. It has no fewer than 20,366 stores in 61 countries.[3]

Supplying the Missing Ingredient

Here's Drucker's colorful name for this: "Hit 'em where they ain't." These words came from baseball Hall of Famer Wee Willie Keeler. At 5 foot 4 inches, Keeler was one of the shortest guys ever to play for a major league team. Despite his height, his .385 career batting average after the 1898 season remains the highest career average in history at season's end for a player with more than 1,000 hits. His strategy was simple: Hit the ball to parts of the field not well protected by opposing players. Wee Willie described this batting style as "Hit 'em where they ain't."

You can use this approach in different ways. The most obvious is by fulfilling a need that a competitor is not fulfilling. However, you can also interpret the strategy as fulfilling a need that no one else in your company or organization is fulfilling. That's an effective approach to success, too, on a more personal level. So, Drucker's insights had a wider application than only the marketing function.

Finding and Occupying an "Ecological Niche"

In nature, an ecological niche is the place or function of a given organism within its ecosystem. Drucker differentiates this approach from the first two points just discussed by contrasting it: positional occupation and control versus grappling with competition or potential competition. According to Drucker, occupying an ecological niche can make a company immune from competition.

The whole point is to be inconspicuous, or to be working in some area that appears to have only limited potential. Drucker recommended three distinct ways for implementing this strategy of occupying an ecological position.

The Toll-Gate Position

Gain a toll-gate position, which means that you control an essential piece of something else that's needed, so that would-be competitors cannot do business without buying what you supply. That's the brilliance of creating a product or service that requires use of another product or service that only you supply, and offering it at low cost. King Gillette and his Blue Blades for the inexpensive razor he sold is a good example of this strategy (see also Chapter 28). He made millions, not on the razors, which he sold at a near loss, but on the blades for those razors.

The Keurig K-Cup machines are another, more recent example. These machines are designed to quickly brew a single cup of coffee or other hot beverage. Everything comes in a prepared, single-serving plastic cup, called a K-Cup. The user simply inserts a K-Cup into the machine, presses a button, and in short order the beverage is ready. If you buy the machine, the toll gate is the use of the K-Cups. In essence, you're paying something like $35 a pound for the coffee, if you compare the amount by weight. Still, people like the convenience and the perfectly measured amount for a good brew.[4]

The Specialty Skill or Specialty Market

The other two ways to occupy a specialized ecological niche is either to have a specialty skill or to work in a specialty market. Life is so focused today that it is not so difficult to acquire a specialty with which few can compete in a specific market.

At one time, a chiropractor was a chiropractor, and a doctor of internal medicine was a doctor of internal medicine. This is no longer an accurate description of either of these professions. For example, if you want a board-certified upper-cervical chiropractor, there are fewer than fifty in all of the United States. One man I know travels hundreds of miles each way several times a year to get these services, flying his own airplane. If you need specialized work, and have a small plane and pilot's license, you might do the same.

If you are familiar with Cesar Millan, the "Dog Whisperer," on television, you are watching an individual who has combined a specialty skill with a specific market. Cesar has mastered the art of handling dogs of all breeds. He knows the individual characteristics of each breed and how to deal with each of them. At the same time, he has limited the practice of his specialty to troubled dog owners. "I train people and rehabilitate dogs" is his tagline.

Changing Economic Characteristics

Drucker's fourth approach is the only one that does not require the introduction of an innovation. Here, the strategy *is* the innovation, since you change certain economic characteristics of what you provide to others.

Years ago, when I studied economics at the University of Chicago, I learned that "utils" was shorthand for "utilities" or "utility," and that *utility* in turn was a measurement of relative customer satisfaction. So, the idea is to change things by increasing customer satisfaction.

For example, the ice cream cone might fall into this category. Although stories abound as to who came up with the idea, the first patent was issued in 1903 to an Italian immigrant by the name of Italo Marchiony. He did not invent ice cream; however, as early as 1896 he came up with the idea of a wafer cup to hold the ice cream. This solved the problem of his customers' breaking or walking off with the glassware that he had used previously to serve the ice cream. He also increased their "utils" by enabling customers to eat the container as well.[5]

The U.S. Post Office made it easier to ship packages by providing free boxes of various sizes for priority shipping and charging a flat rate according to box size instead of by weight. Their "utils" advantage is described in the slogan, "If it fits, it ships." These five words dramatically increased sales by changing how their service was viewed by potential customers.

Creating "utils" is easy. All you need to do is ask yourself what would truly make things easier or better for your customers or for the other organizations in your company that you support.

* * *

Want to be successful? Try following Drucker's four approaches to entrepreneurial success. They'll work whether you are an external entrepreneur or a manager trying to perform at your peak potential.

CHAPTER TWENTY-SIX

If You Conduct Marketing Research, Conduct It Right

Marketing research is taught in every business school. There are thousands of marketing research firms in every big city, and an awful lot of them in small towns, too. So everyone knows that you *must* do marketing research. However, Drucker uncovered a startling fact. Much of this research is wasted, misinterpreted, or misused, and probably shouldn't even be attempted. His advice was: Better not to do it at all than to do it wrong!

As has been mentioned in earlier chapters, IBM, for years the leading manufacturer of huge corporate computers, researched the market for personal computers long before Steve Jobs and Steve Wozniak came along. IBM was neither a novice nor a patsy, by anyone's measurement. They did a thorough job and their marketing research cost a bundle. After much work, numbers crunching, and analysis, the IBM researchers concluded, with little margin for error, that if IBM invested the millions necessary to develop a personal computer for home use, the total number that could be sold would amount to no more than 1,000 units a year. So overwhelming and so convincing were the marketing researchers that they were able to dissuade management from this terrible waste of time, money, and resources. IBM dropped the whole personal computer idea.

This left the way open for Jobs and Wozniak, of course, who had done no marketing research at all. Yet they founded a billion-dollar industry that changed the world. Steve Jobs later said, "A lot of times people don't know what they want until you show it to them." The Wright Brothers would have agreed. They had a terrible time marketing their airplane to the U.S. Army. It took years, even after they made their first flight in 1903.

Drucker had said it many times before: "One cannot do market research for something genuinely new. One cannot do market research for something that is not yet on the market."[1] He argued that there was always risk with something new, that it was always a gamble, but that this risk could be reduced or minimized. He considered marketing research as conducted by most of us as the wrong prescription for doing this, however.

Reducing Risk with Reality Testing

How can you reduce the risk if you don't do marketing research? One way to lower the risk in this gamble is "the test of reality."[2] In other words, get something out into the market and see what happens. Yes, in a way this is some sort of test marketing. However, it needn't be expensive or dependent on sophisticated numbers crunching.

Dr. Richard Buskirk, who headed up the entrepreneurship program at the University of Southern California for a number of years, said much the same thing: "I tell my students not to waste time and money on marketing research. Get out there in the marketplace and start trying to sell your product. You'll find out soon enough whether you're going to be successful." I suspect Drucker would have classified Dr. Buskirk's approach as "reality testing," though perhaps limited to projects requiring only a small investment.

When Lee Iacocca thought about reintroducing a convertible into a market that had seen few convertibles over the preceding generation, he called a meeting of his design and production staff at Chrysler. He told them, "Cut the top off one of our standard sedans," and he gave his staff a day to get the job done. The next day, the team met with Iacocca to present the plans and drawings using a current model, but with new tooling to incorporate a feature that would fold the top into the trunk. The plans included cost estimates and approval points. They had worked all night to get this done in only twenty-four hours, and they were pretty proud of their accomplishment. "No," cried Iacocca. "You don't understand. I want you to cut the top off of one of our cars and have it ready for me this afternoon."

According to corporate legend, if Iacocca did any quantitative analysis in this research, it was that he counted how many people waved as he drove this ad hoc "convertible" around town.[3] This, Drucker would agree, was "reality testing" at its finest.

Along the same lines would be the introduction of a limited amount of product into the market or into a limited geographical area. Drucker's argument was that too much effort in marketing research is expended on complicated questions that are meaningless when, as Steve Jobs said—words to the effect—it's difficult to fully explain a product that doesn't exist. I am reminded of an early advertisement for thermometers that were to be inserted in the ear to measure body temperature. The ad read: "What do you think they thought when patients were told where they were to insert the original thermometer for home measurement of temperature?" In any case, it's not the marketer who defines a new product or service, it's always the *customer.*

Even a Product's Use Is Defined by Its Customers

DuPont introduced the product Kevlar in the early 1970s. This is a super-cloth whose fibers have five times the tensile strength of steel. The marketers thought it would make an excellent substitute for the steel reinforcement in heavy-duty tires. It did, but it made even better fragmentation-protective body armor. When impregnated for rigidity to protect against blunt trauma, it also was excellent for the protective helmets worn by ground combatants. Those helmets are used by U.S. troops today, and they provide much more protection than the old "steel pots" worn by soldiers to protect the head during World War II and in Korea and Vietnam.

Drucker warned that marketers who are introducing new products or services should start with the assumption that people might find other uses never imagined when the products were designed and introduced. I recall that, as a West Point cadet, the most effective way to get a quick shine on shoes was with 5-Day Deodorant Pads. And this offbeat use wasn't confined to West Point. A professor of nutrition at the University of California, Davis, recently recounted his ROTC days at UCLA: "I learned quickly how to use 5-Day Deodorant Pads for that mirror finish on my shoes that was required for passing inspection."[4]

I don't know whether anyone from the company manufacturing those deodorant pads ever tried to exploit this additional market. They might have even gotten a little upset had they known of this use—but our shoes must have smelled pretty good. The point is that this kind of thing happens. Drucker related once how German chemist Alfred Einhorn, the inventor of the anesthetic drug Novocain, went all around Germany in the early 1900s trying to convince dentists not to use his product (see also Chapter 29). That's because it was intended for use by medical doctors, not dentists. We all know how that turned out.

What You Need to Know About Customers

Marketers are on the right track, according to Drucker, when they seek to learn who their customers and potential customers are, what they buy, where they are, what they read or watch on television, and so on. However, he found that few marketers ask perhaps the most important question of all: *What do customers and potential customers value?*[5] He stressed this, again and again. It doesn't matter what the marketer thinks is important or what is or is not a competitive advantage. Rather, it's what the customer thinks is an advantage of the product or service.

What does the customer value? What the marketer defines as quality and how the customer defines quality may be entirely different. This is why it's important to do some research outside your regular channels, looking at companies and products that are not your direct competition.

Indirect Competition Shouldn't Be Neglected

Indirect competition is a claimant on your potential customers' disposable dollars for what they value. Sufferers who take pills to cure headaches want fast, effective, long-lasting relief. So, too, marketers compete head-to-head on this basis and boast about these qualities in their drug products to "cure" headaches. However, vitamin supplements are growing by leaps and bounds as a treatment for headaches, as are other competitive methods, from acupuncture to meditation. What customers *really* want is to avoid the pain, and therefore something that does this well is what they really value. If a method is effective in preventing or curing headaches, people will use it, no matter what it may be.

Until I was fourteen years old, I suffered from terrible headaches. Then one day I heard on the radio that any headache could be stopped cold without drugs of any kind. The year was 1951, and my father hadn't yet agreed that we needed a television. (Yes, I'm that old.) This could be done simply by pressing gently and simultaneously at the mid-forehead and at the base of the skull in the neck. Suffering with a bad headache even as I listened, I immediately applied this advice. Guess what? My headache vanished, and I haven't had one since. Before you rush to try this cure, however, I should tell you that, though I tried it dozens of times later, with many other people, it never worked again with anyone else—with this one exception.

I was on a flight from Washington, D.C., to Los Angeles. My assigned seat was next to a boy of about ten or eleven, who was in some agony and had a wet washcloth on his head and was emitting sounds of discomfort. Before I could ask what was wrong, a stewardess rushed up with a replacement washcloth. She explained that the boy had a severe headache, but because he was traveling alone and was underage, she wasn't permitted to give him any form of headache medication. The stewardess mumbled some words of encouragement to the sufferer and rushed off.

I told him that I didn't know whether the technique I had used successfully years before would work, but he was welcome to try it if he wished. I explained what to do. He did what I told him and an immediate smile appeared on his face. "Thanks, it's completely gone," he said as he removed the washcloth. About that time, the stewardess came up with another wet washcloth. She started to make some sympathetic remarks, but he told her, "It's okay. I don't need anything now. He fixed it for me." He pointed toward me. The stewardess immediately launched into a tirade, threatening me with arrest and stating that it was against the law to give even minor headache pills without the parents' permission. I explained what had happened and the boy backed up my story, but you could see by the look on her face that she didn't believe a word either of us said.

In any case, Drucker recommended that marketing researchers be most concerned about *indirect* competition. And if that method of headache cure could be made to work more reliably, the makers of headache pills would really have something to worry about.

* * *

Peter Drucker advised doing marketing research, but doing it in the right way and focusing on doing the important, relevant issues—not the less important, minor aspects of the market or market matters. We don't do marketing research for statistics; we do it to give us real insight. Shall we introduce a new personal computer or a drugless headache cure? Do a reality test.

CHAPTER TWENTY-SEVEN

Be Careful in Using a Bribe

Before you get too upset about the title of this chapter, please consider common definitions of the word *bribe*. These include:

1. Something, such as money or a favor, offered or given to a person to influence that person's views or conduct

2. Something serving to influence or persuade

We talked about bribery in Chapter 1. This is bribery in a different context. Drucker identified several ways of bribing prospects, which he called "buying customers." Despite their popularity, he did not recommend using any of these ways. He wrote that you could price a product so low that there was little, if any, profit. The idea behind this strategy was to persuade a prospect to make a current purchase in the hope that he would buy again at the full price in the future. This made severe underpricing an acceptable alternative to many other pricing strategies. But customers often expect to continue paying the lower price.

Or, you could try to buy customers by offering them unwarranted discounts, cash bonuses, low- or no-interest financing, or some other incentive to purchase. Yes, these tactics might work, but you must be cautious, because these incentives typically work for a limited time only, and then they might result in unwarranted permanent consequences.

Customers Expect Bribes to Continue

Some years ago, a friend of mine, who was a young accountant working for the health-care organization Blue Cross, did a little moonlighting during tax season. To break into this established market, he charged the bargain price of $75 an hour, when the going rate in his geographical area was about twice that. This method is sometimes called "penetration pricing." But if marketers do this, they need to be careful. Did this moonlighting accountant get clients? Absolutely! Since he was employed full-time, he considered this once-a-year part-time work pure gravy. Being an excellent accountant, his seasonal practice grew every year.

Ten years later, he had the opportunity to purchase a private accounting practice and leave his full-time employer. The clientele of his former part-time business then made up a significant percentage of his new independent practice. But this presented a problem. He had two classes of clients: one group paying $150 an hour and the other paying $75 an hour.

This young accountant assumed that his part-time clientele knew they had been getting a tremendously good deal before, and maybe they did know. However, when he contacted them to announce his new practice and gave them the news that they would now be charged $150 an hour, every one of those clients dropped him. More than a few were angry. Most went to other tax accountants, some not as experienced. They had no idea whether or not these other accountants were as good as their former accountant, yet they happily paid these others more than $75 an hour—a few even $150 an hour. They just wouldn't pay their former low-priced accountant this amount. This example confirms Drucker's warning about this type of bribery.

Car Companies Show Why Drucker Was Concerned

Peter Drucker used the automobile industry as a big-business example to show the reason for his concern about this bribery. First, he focused on the Hyundai Excel. When Hyundai made its initial foray into the American market, it entered with a bang by charging an eye-opening low price, helping it be voted one of the best new products, listed as such in *Fortune* magazine. The Excel set a record for first-year imports and its cumulative production exceeded 1 million within two years. Hyundai had the fastest growth of any automobile in history.

The problem was that, to accomplish this success, Hyundai had pulled out all the stops and had also shaved its costs to the bone to enable a pricing bribe. Suddenly, the car disappeared from the market. Quality problems played a part. However, as Drucker noted, a manufacturer must have sufficient profits to reinvest in its business, including enough money to correct quality problems in design and on the production line. Hyundai lacked sufficient profits owing to its pricing bribe.[1]

U.S. manufacturers made the same mistake when they were losing market share to the Japanese. The "Big Three" auto companies offered all sorts of customer bribes. Did they work? Yes, they did. In every case and for every program, sales went up. The problem was that when each offer expired, the sales nosedived to a lower level than before the incentive because the companies attracted few, if any, new or permanent customers. In short, bribery has a limited life expectancy and may cause negative consequences. Overall, both GM and Chrysler lost substantial shares to the Japanese, while Ford was barely able to maintain its position.[2]

Think Before You Bribe

Before any marketer decides to buy customers through bribery, that marketer needs to reflect on the objective and how the results are going to play in the marketplace. A sales incentive, or any other strategy for buying customers, is supposed to allow you to temporarily lower the price without affecting your product's image or your ability to raise the price again later. The problem is that this assumption is frequently false. If your customers or prospects always seek the lowest price, and that is the primary reason for their buying from you, you might just as well lower your price permanently now.

Customers and prospects know you are not granting discounts because you like their looks or it is a holiday. Through incentives, you can buy customers and you will increase sales temporarily. But if buying customers is your primary differential advantage, then as soon as your discounting or other incentive has expired or is ended, your customer is going to go elsewhere to find the lowest price again.

I don't think that Drucker was against programs designed to accomplish a specific objective over a very short term. However, you always need to ask the question, "Why aren't we getting more sales at our current pricing?" Or, if your objective is to break into an established market, you need to access exactly how you can do this and avoid the trap of being in a low-priced niche (as our part-time accountant did).

When Is a Bribe Not a Bribe?

During World War I, thirty-eight-year-old Douglas MacArthur was a brigadier general. He had been in combat for some time, but had just assumed command of a new brigade in France. After planning an important attack, he went forward and waited in the trenches with the battalion that was going to lead the way. This battalion had never been in combat. He could see that the young battalion commander was nervous. And no wonder. He was required to lead the entire battalion "over the top"—up and outside of the trench that protected them—and attack the enemy head-on to gain the objective.

MacArthur called the battalion commander to him. "Major," he said, "when the signal comes to go over the top, if you go first, before your men, your battalion will follow you." The major himself recognized that his leading from the front would greatly increase the battalion's likelihood of success.

Normally, a battalion commander is not supposed to lead an attack from the front. The military tactics manuals say that a battalion commander should be with the group, following the company in the lead making the attack. That way, he is not personally as vulnerable and can better control the attack as it unfolds. But MacArthur knew that there are times when the rules must be violated, and that this was one time.

"I will not order you to do this," continued MacArthur. "In the front of the battalion, every German gun will be trained on you. It will be very dangerous and require a great deal of courage. However, if you do it, you will earn the Distinguished Service Cross and I will see that you get it."

MacArthur was saying that if the young major would do as he suggested, the major would receive a high military decoration. By definition, this was a bribe. MacArthur stated what needed to be done to maximize the accomplishment of an important goal. This would require the major to risk his life to an extraordinary degree. In a sense, rather than giving the major an order, MacArthur was stating a promised reward for the act that he wanted the major to perform.

MacArthur then stepped back and looked the major over for several long moments. He stepped forward again. "I see you are going to do it. So, you will have the Distinguished Service Cross now." In so saying, MacArthur unpinned a Distinguished Service Cross from his own uniform and pinned it on the uniform of the major. That was an extraordinary act on his part and virtually guaranteed that the major would accept his bribe.

When the signal came to "go over the top" and begin the attack, the major, who was proudly wearing that Distinguished Service Cross, ran out in front of his troops. As MacArthur had forecast, the major's troops followed and, as a result, they were successful in securing their objective.[3] In a sense, this was a successful bribe. However, it was successful for this one time only, and could not, and probably would not, be used again.

This example illustrates Drucker's warning in an entirely different context. Call them what you will, the use of bribes, either in leadership or in marketing, must be carefully considered in advance. Yes, they can be effective, but only for the short term and only when the objectives and consequences are weighed carefully before the decision is made.

* * *

If you are going to bribe customers through your pricing or other incentives, you must be certain that this is for the attainment of a short-term, temporary goal, and that you have thought through an exit strategy for the bribe so that you can get back to the price that should be paid for your goods or services. If not, like Drucker's automobile example or my young accountant friend, you may be in serious trouble.

CHAPTER TWENTY-EIGHT

There Are No Irrational Customers, Only Irrational Marketers

Value is a strong influence on what customers purchase. When you have what the customers value, they buy from you. Price is one, and only one, measurement of value.[1] Yet some marketers wonder why customers would *ever* buy a more expensive product when a cheaper one of equal or sometimes even greater quality is available. These marketers say that such customers are "irrational." But Peter Drucker maintained that irrational customers don't exist. However, he thought that the stubborn belief that customers who don't buy when the marketer thinks they should may itself be irrational. So maybe this means that a marketer who believes this may be a little irrational. Let's take a closer look.

The Easy Answers

At times, so-called irrational customers are fairly easy to explain. When there is limited information about a product and the potential customers have no experience with it, it is perfectly rational to assume that the most expensive product is the one of the highest quality and therefore worth more. We have all seen this. For example, we know nothing about headache cures, so we select the most expensive drug on the market.

Or, perhaps through shrewd advertising, we perceive that a higher-priced product may be better or of higher quality than a cheaper brand, when this is not the case. This is one reason that many marketing experts suggest that your pricing be *congruent*. That is, you should charge a higher price for a product that is of higher quality or has more desirable features, even if you could charge less.

Similarly, if a price reduction fails to increase sales, maybe the price reduction is too small relative to the original price to attract much attention. Or, other factors may be considered far more important at the time, such as a supplier's reputation for reliability or of available delivery times.

In every case, there are logical reasons for the buyer's decision to pay more—even for what the marketer might consider less value. Drucker concluded that customers are never irrational, and when they make surprising decisions in the marketplace, the marketers should examine those purchases from the customer's perspective to uncover the real reasons behind them, so they can be dealt with successfully in the future.

Start with the Customer's Perspective

The marketer must start with what customers want to buy, rather than with what suppliers want to sell. Did you know that for many years foreigners saw more images of one particular American than any other? It was not the image of an American president, a famous general, or one of our Founding Fathers. And I'm not talking about the days when John Wayne represented America to all moviegoers around the world. Rather, this was a man who sold safety razors.

He wasn't the first to sell a safety razor, and he didn't invent the safety razor or their blades. His razor wasn't any better than anyone else's. He did price it very reasonably, and—catch this—it was more expensive to produce than the price he charged. The man in question was King Gillette. His picture was on the package of every razor and every blade that he sold. And he sold them by the millions, all over the world.

Though he lost money on every razor he sold, Gillette more than made up for the loss on the blades he sold afterwards. Every blade cost him less than one cent to make, and he sold each for five cents. That's a nice markup, but it was really a win-win because it benefited his customers, too. Since the blade could be used at least six times, buyers got a shave for less than one cent. That was one-tenth of the going rate for a shave in a barbershop in those days—though, as the old seven-note musical couplet informed, a shave with a haircut was "two bits," slang for twenty-five cents in the United States around the turn of the twentieth century.

What Customers Really Want

Gillette understood his customers. He priced his razors at about 10 percent of the price of his competitors' safety razors, and he positioned his buyers to enjoy a tremendous cost savings at the same time. He realized that customers were not buying either razors or blades. That's just what his company manufactured. The customers were buying shaves.[2]

Recently, I saw another example of this viewpoint in the solar energy business. Solar cells have been around for quite a while, and consumers are well aware that there is money to be saved from both the free energy from the sun and via federal tax rebates for buying energy-saving devices. In some areas of the country, arrays of solar cells sit atop practically every rooftop.

The problem, however, has been the large investment required, which could easily be in the thousands of dollars for the solar cells and their installation. Just as King Gillette realized that people were interested in buying shaves, not razors or blades, at least one company has seen that customers want energy, not solar cells or energy-saving systems. Though money at the time was short, they began offering free installation of the solar cells and the ancillary system. The big difference was that the customers wouldn't own the cells or ancillary equipment; the solar energy company would maintain them and retain ownership. The customer would pay only for the solar energy used, which is significantly less than the amount paid for the use of electrical energy. That's smart marketing, and it follows perfectly Drucker's view of customer rationality.

In other words, this is what pricing is all about. Any marketer willing to use his customers as the basis of his pricing can acquire industry leadership almost without risk. Of course, to enable you to do this, you also need to look at cost—but not until you start with the price and determine what it is from the customer's perspective. This was a major issue with Drucker: you determine price first, and only then turn to cost. This, by extension, takes us to such things as chain costing.

The Concept of Chain Costing

Got a favorite gasoline station only five miles across town, where the price is 5 cents a gallon less than the gas station one block away? You may be better off paying the higher cents. But look at the figures.

Let's say your car gets 15 miles a gallon while driving in town. To get there and back to your starting point is 10 miles. If the gasoline costs $3.50 a gallon at the cheaper gas station, this 10-mile drive will use two-thirds of a gallon, or $2.33. If your car holds 15 gallons, you will have saved 75 cents on a tankful. Not bad. However, your drive was a net loss of $1.58 ($2.33 – $0.75). But wait. If your little trip across town took 15 minutes and was made during work hours, you also should factor that time in. How much do you make on an hourly basis? If your salary and benefits total $100,000 annually and you have 2,000 productive work hours in a year, that's another negative $12.50. Now your trip has cost you over $14! And I'm leaving out wear and tear on your tires and engine, insurance, and so on.

In the city where I live, one of the local radio stations announces the cheapest gasoline in town. It's always a few cents cheaper than elsewhere. But, heck, even if the gasoline were a dollar a gallon less, I'd barely break even on a fill-up. This, then, is the importance of chain costing, which implies simply that you need to consider all of the relevant costs in the chain.

The importance of looking at the entire economic chain is hardly a new idea. This concept was first expressed by economist Alfred Marshall in the 1890s.[3] Marshall was no slouch. He was the person who brought the basic concepts of supply and demand, marginal utility, and costs of production into one coherent theory. Unfortunately, many practitioners thought his work exactly that—pure theory with no practical application. Drucker thought differently.

The notion of chain costing is easily applied to your total costs for producing a particular product or service, but it may also reflect the costs that your customers are paying. The latter costs may or may not be recognized or understood by the customers (witness the attraction of saving a few cents at the gasoline pump). But as a smart marketer, you should understand the concept when setting prices if you are to take advantage of these factors to present your customers with rational reasons for buying.

Chain costing may also help you understand the advantages, as well as the challenges, of vertical integration of your product's process, from planning and design to post-sales actions—whether or not its results are seen by your consumers. To put it in Drucker's terms, "What matters in the marketplace is the economic reality, the costs of the entire process, regardless of who owns what."[4]

Costs Will Change Down the Road

We are frequently too quick to assume that present costs will last forever. Drucker liked to point out that smarter marketers and price setters take over our markets by looking at them differently each time. That's why the United States didn't hold on to the market for fax machines, even though the machines were invented here. The Japanese didn't look at the costs of producing the initial numbers of fax machines, they looked at the numbers of machines that would be sold several years in the future. Ironically, the process of using a learning or experience curve to develop future costs and apply them to today was also developed in the United States.

This type of forecasting came about in the late 1930s, owing to Boeing's production of the B-17 bomber, when analysts at Wright-Patterson Air Force Base realized that every time its total aircraft production doubled, its labor decreased by 10 to 15 percent and its costs went down. Subsequent empirical studies from other industries and products yielded other measurable values. Nevertheless, the curve of decline could be determined and used to predict future costs. In fact, the method was good enough to be employed throughout World War II and is still required of those bidding on government defense contracts today.

Drucker's message, thus, was that price should determine cost, rather than the other way around. And once you have the price, it is only prudent to look at the costs to ensure that the product can be sold profitably. But you also need to consider all other aspects of costs, including the fact that as you produce more of anything the costs of that production will decline. His overriding lesson, however, was that customers are not irrational, as pointed out at the beginning of this chapter. If they aren't buying your product, but are buying someone else's product, there is a rational reason that you need to uncover and correct.

CHAPTER TWENTY-NINE

Where the Best Innovations Come From

Wouldn't it be nice if a genie arose from a magic lamp and revealed the richest source of innovation for profitability in your business? With just one such innovation you could make a fortune for yourself or your employer. Peter F. Drucker was not a genie, but he was a genius. So respected was Drucker that even today, almost ten years after his death, there are Drucker Societies all over the world that meet once a year at his old school in Claremont, California. They are still teaching and applying his business principles.

I had the good fortune to be the first graduate of Drucker's Ph.D. program, and perhaps even more fortunate today in being president of a graduate school that teaches his principles as part of every MBA course. So I can pass on to you what Drucker said was the richest source of innovation, just as if he were a genie and you had a magic lamp calling him forth.

The Richest Source of Innovation

Drucker wrote that the "unexpected" was the richest source of opportunity for successful innovation. Unfortunately, unexpected occurrences are not only many times neglected but also are frequently actively rejected. As a result, they are never exploited as innovations. As noted earlier, German chemist Alfred Einhorn became distressed when dentists began using his anesthetic drug Novocain, which he intended to be used only by medical doctors. He was so upset that he refused to sell it to dentists, and he traveled up and down Germany spending a lot of money to discourage this "incorrect" use until a smarter entrepreneur took over and made millions by selling Novocain to dentists, its most common use today.

Example: When R.H. Macy's Tried to Dump Their Appliance Business

After World War II, appliance sales at R.H. Macy & Co. suddenly and mysteriously began to increase dramatically. Not only did sales increase but profit margins also were significantly higher on appliances than on fashion goods, Macy's flagship product line. Plus, unlike fashion goods, for appliances there were almost no returns and no pilferage. If that weren't enough, customers who came in the store to buy appliances frequently stayed to buy products in other Macy departments, so sales of fashion goods and other classes of Macy's product line all increased.

You would expect Macy's to celebrate and exploit this unexpected occurrence as an immediate and profitable innovation and to put additional resources into its appliance business. Yet this experienced retailer, the biggest department store around, not only failed to take advantage of this potential innovation but it also did everything possible to make these unexpected, profitable results go away.

When its fashion goods failed to increase as a percentage of total sales even after Macy's tried everything to make this happen, the department store actually began a campaign to restrict appliance sales.

"We'll teach those stubborn appliance people how to lose money" almost seemed to be its mantra. Competitor Bloomingdale's saw the same thing happen in its store. However, Bloomingdale's not only built on its appliance sales but it also built a whole new market around a new housewares department. Previously, Bloomingdale's had been a weak number four in the marketplace. Its successful innovation based on these unexpected results, however, soon catapulted it into a very strong number two position.

What caused Macy's strange behavior? Everyone in the industry "knew" that in a well-run department store, fashion should produce 70 percent of total sales. But those errant appliance sales were providing three-fifths of total Macy's revenue! This had to be stopped! Obviously, nobody at Macy's had considered Drucker's principle that "what everybody knows is usually wrong."

The chairman of Macy's came to the conclusion that if fashion sales couldn't be increased, appliance sales would have to be reduced. And so he set out to do just that. Not such good thinking, Mr. Chairman!

Is the Classical Glass of Water Half Empty?

You know the classic question about optimism: Is the glass of water half full or half empty? That all depends on how you look at things, of course. Moreover, a person's mood, values, beliefs, or what has been seen or known previously all affect one's perception of possibility.

How can you take advantage of perception as a source of innovation? At one time, a rip in clothing was cause for the quality inspector to reject the product and throw it out, or if the tear was minor, it might be sold at a significant discount. However, the late 1960s saw the onset of the Hippie Generation, with young people wearing clothing that was often intentionally ripped. Almost overnight, worn-out, faded, frayed, and, yes, even ripped jeans became status symbols preferred by many younger prospective buyers.

In response to what was perceived as desirable, jean manufacturers began to make clothing that intentionally resembled clothing once considered damaged, suitable only to be thrown away or donated to worthy organizations for recycling. This is an example of exactly what Peter Drucker meant by an unexpected occurrence.

There undoubtedly was risk involved in producing large quantities of ripped, frayed, and faded jeans and then to market them to an unsuspecting public. But once a market arose for clothes that had been discarded in the past, jean manufacturers would have been foolish to ignore it.

Sometimes the Market Talks to You

Drucker's advice was that when something unexpected happened, the entrepreneur should immediately examine that closely. Indeed, the market may be giving you the richest of all sources of innovation. I've mentioned earlier in the book about my friend Joe Cossman, the well-known entrepreneur. Cossman had created a sprinkler system based on simply making holes in a plastic hose. He saw an unexpected increase in orders from poultry farms rather than from the households or gardeners that he had anticipated. He looked into this unexpected development and found that the poultry farms were using these hose sprinklers as inexpensive air conditioners for their chicken pens. Cossman did not refuse to sell to them; instead, this opened up a new market for his product, which he quickly exploited.

The modern bikini was another unexpected innovation. It was introduced in 1946 by Louis Réard, an automotive engineer who was managing his mother's lingerie boutique near Paris, and his partner in the venture, the fashion designer Jacques Heim. Heim noticed the increasingly revealing two-piece bathing suits that women were wearing and the more liberal laws and attitudes toward skimpy clothing in France. The partners named their new swimsuit after Bikini Atoll, where the United States had tested the atomic bomb. They chose the name because they believed that the revealing swimwear would cause as much of a stir worldwide as had the atomic bomb, which had been dropped on Japan the year before.

They advertised their bikini as "smaller than the smallest swimsuit." At first, they were unable to find a model willing to be photographed wearing it (and this was France, known to have the most liberal dress codes for women!). They ended up hiring a nude dancer from a Paris casino, who was not afraid to wear it. Today, we all know that their innovation paid off. The bikini in its many varied forms is a billion-dollar business—and not just in France, either.

What You Should Do When Strange Things Happen

As mentioned above, managers looking for new innovations should study every unexpected outcome or occurrence. In doing so, they need to ask four basic questions:

1. What would it mean if we exploited this development? That is, what are the short-term costs and benefits of developing this unexpected result into an opportunity?

2. Where could it lead us?

3. What would we have to do to convert it into an opportunity? In other words, how would we convert the unexpected result into a profitable product or system for the company?

4. What would be the plan for doing this? What resources would be needed? What would it cost? What would the timing look like? What would be the approximate quantified results of the investment?

Peter Drucker not only told us that the unexpected was the richest source of innovation, but instructed exactly what to do to take advantage of this innovation—follow Bloomingdale's actions: When sales are surprisingly blooming, embrace the unexpected success.

Have you thrown away any potential billion-dollar innovations by ignoring the unexpected results?

CHAPTER THIRTY

Drucker's Theory of Abandonment

Jack Welch began his twenty-year tenure as CEO of General Electric in 1981. Welch was the youngest CEO in GE's history. This also was the start of his legend as one of the leading CEOs of the twentieth century. When Welch became CEO, the company's market value was about $12 billion. When he left, it was worth more than twenty-five times that figure. GE saw the largest increases in both its sales and its profits under his leadership.

According to Welch, two simple questions from Peter Drucker initiated and helped to propel GE to these amazing accomplishments and to establish his own stature as a business executive of heroic accomplishments. The first question was, "If GE wasn't already in a particular business, would you enter it today?" The second was, "If the answer is no, what are you going to do about it?"

Welch said Drucker's questions led him to shed less profitable and underperforming businesses. His implementation of responses to Drucker's two questions resulted in an order that any GE business that was neither number one nor runner-up in its market, and that had no chance of attaining this status, would be sold or liquidated.[1,2] This freed up resources, which allowed GE to concentrate on businesses that would soon dominate their markets and become hugely successful.

The GE story is a prime example of Drucker's theory of abandonment. He did not originate it during his consulting engagement with GE; rather, it had been his advice given in his book *Managing by Results*, published in 1964, almost twenty years earlier. Of course, the GE results are also a powerful testimony to Welch's ability to apply Drucker's theory correctly and to implement his own solution for a phenomenal success.[3]

Drucker's Systematic Process of Abandonment

Drucker's concept of abandonment was so challenging, both psychologically and in real terms, that it had to be instilled at the molecular level of an organization. To move ahead, an organization had to be prepared to abandon everything it had been doing at the same time as it devoted itself to creating something new in order to move ahead. This approach required someone like Welch, with the determination and moral courage to take action, especially since abandonment required action in the face of significant previous success (or what appeared to be success at the time of abandonment). If that weren't enough, the abandonment had to be executed simultaneously with continuous improvement and exploitation of past successes, wherever possible, as well as with innovation.[4]

There was no getting around it. A proposal for a major new effort had to spell out in detail what of the old effort must be abandoned and how this should be accomplished.[5] No wonder Welch was disparagingly called "Neutron Jack" as he ruthlessly sold off GE companies and forced employees, both workers and managers, to move to areas of the company where they were needed—or to leave the corporation altogether.[6]

Rethinking: The Prelude to Abandonment

In an essay entitled *"Really* Reinventing Government," Drucker analyzed the thought that must take place as a preamble to abandonment.[7] This notion of rethinking should be applied to reinventing anything, including a company's products or policies. It must involve a review of the organization's ongoing programs that require resources of any kind to continue. Drucker recognized that this would mean a long list of activities, programs, or products to examine.

The most successful entities, at the top of the list, should then be given even more resources to further exploit their success. As in the example of GE, these roughly correspond to businesses that are both profitable and the leaders in their markets. Those at the bottom of the list have to be discarded. Those in between might be retained if they showed promise, but if so, they probably need to be modified significantly.

Farewell to Good Intentions

Drucker noted that corporate policies tend to rank programs and activities according to good intentions. That is, a business might be profitable; everyone hopes these profits will increase and the business will grow. This was true for GE's businesses when Welch became CEO. But rather than having good intentions, rethinking ranks all businesses according to performance, both present and achievable.[8]

This ranking is somewhat analogous to the Boston Consulting Group's well-known categorization of businesses into shooting stars, cash cows, question marks, and dogs. However, there is a major difference. Under Drucker, there is no sense in retaining a business, even a cash cow, if its performance does not warrant doing that. The simple question is how high to set the bar.

Abandonment Is Both a Necessity and an Opportunity

During rethinking, the manager conducts categorization. The rethinking prior to abandonment is not just for purposes of constructing a list; it also helps you identify opportunities as products (or businesses, or anything else). Existing businesses, therefore, are divided into three categories:[9]

1. A high-priority ongoing group where there is a significant opportunity to achieve extraordinary results

2. A high-priority group where the opportunity is in abandonment

3. A large group of mediocre items for which neither efforts to exploit nor abandonment are likely to lead to significant results

As noted previously, whenever a business or operation is abandoned, this frees up resources: money, personnel, facilities, equipment, and time to develop new opportunities or to take advantage of older ones with higher potential. Drucker called this sorting into areas of priority "push priorities." He noted that they were easy to identify: Push priorities are opportunities where the results have the potential to pay back their investments many times over.[10]

There are other advantages to abandonment, too. Psychologically, abandonment makes it acceptable to search for and find replacements for former businesses or products. You don't have to confront the sacred cow. According to Drucker, abandonment also renders an "existing business entrepreneurial"—one that can "work *today* on the products, services, processes, and technologies that will make a difference tomorrow."[11] Finally, abandonment facilitates change management. Extending Drucker's principle that the best way to predict the future is to create it, the most effective way to manage change is to create change yourself.[12]

Finding the Right Candidates for Help or Abandonment

Any rethinking list, or more extensive analysis in a systematic abandonment review process, will result in pointing to certain areas that deserve priority attention. These are the push priorities mentioned in the last section and they include:

- Identifying tomorrow's breadwinners and sleepers. Breadwinners are those candidates who routinely produce positive benefits. Sleepers, which Drucker termed "Cinderellas," are those candidates who have hidden potential.

- Making development efforts to replace tomorrow's breadwinners, "the day after tomorrow."

- Recognizing important new knowledge and distribution channels.

- Reducing high support costs, high control costs, and waste.

The candidates for help are usually obvious—they need resources to take advantage of a potential that clearly exists. Examples of these would be Welch's profitable GE businesses that were market leaders. The candidates for abandonment are equally obvious, including those for which investment is primarily managerial ego, unjustified specialties, unnecessary support activities, waste that can be almost effortlessly dispensed with, and, of course, yesterday's breadwinners. Finally, whenever the cost of incremental acquisition is more than one-half the probable return, abandonment should be seriously considered.[13]

Drucker summarized a lifetime of observation of the abandonment concept by stating three cases where "the right action is always outright abandonment."[14]

1. If a product, service, process, and so on still has "a few good years left"

2. If the only argument for keeping it is that it is "fully written off"

3. If a new candidate is being stunted or neglected because an old, declining product is being maintained

The Criterion for Abandonment

Drucker provided no criteria for abandonment because the criteria are almost unlimited. However, he did provide some clues. For example, in decision making, Drucker recommended looking at what he called "boundary conditions." These are specifications regarding intended objectives, minimal attainment goals, and other considerations that must be satisfied for an organization to remain viable. By inference, these boundary conditions are markers for the development of criteria for abandonment.[15]

Drucker added that budgeting, the most widely used management tool, provides a forum for evaluating and analyzing the existing situation. Thus, budgeting should be used along with other quantitative and non-quantitative measurements and controls in reviewing which candidates qualify for abandonment.

Implementing Abandonment

Of course, a plan for abandonment should be complete with specific objectives; numbers of people needed with various capabilities; and the tools, money, information, and other resources required for completion of the implementation, along with unambiguous deadlines for reaching certain stages. Drucker noted that this "how" of abandonment was of no less importance than the "what."

Abandonment is not without its cost. For example, Welch's abandonment of some GE businesses required displacement of more than 100,000 employees, as he discarded underperforming businesses and acquired new ones. However, the abandonment process Welch initiated ultimately benefited the remaining employees, GE's customers, its stockholders, and most importantly, society. The latter is true because society is hurt when it continues to allocate workers and managers to no longer fully productive activities, but it is benefited when these valuable resources are reallocated to the best possible opportunities in an organization.

CHAPTER THIRTY-ONE

The Mysteries of Supply-Side Innovation

After some very deep thinking, Peter Drucker concluded that any business organization had just two basic functions: innovation and marketing. After a closer examination of innovation, he decided that innovation itself should be further divided into two categories. One category was demand-side innovation, in which the innovator has a definite objective or problem he is trying to solve. That is, the innovation is demanded by the need. The other category was supply-side innovation, in which the innovator stumbles on something unexpectedly.[1]

"Supply side" is a term of economics. Its origins go back to an eighteenth-century French businessman and economist, Jean-Baptiste Say. But it was best explained by John Maynard Keynes, known for his Keynesian economics, as "supply creates its own demand."[2] In terms of innovation, this means that one becomes aware of the existence, value, and use of something, and that awareness then helps create the innovation.

About ten years ago, I was giving a seminar on marketing in southwest China. I wanted to surprise the attendees with a product that I thought would be unknown and strange in China. I took the product from my briefcase and held it above my head. Before I could utter a word, almost in unison the fifty-plus attendees—none of whom spoke fluent English—shouted out: "Silly Putty!"

The beginnings of this product date back about seventy years, to the early days of World War II. Rubber, which was essential for the war effort, came from rubber trees grown on islands in the Southwest Pacific, which were under Japanese control. In desperation, the United States started a massive program to develop a synthetic rubber. Now, if there had been positive results to this effort, it would have constituted a demand-side innovation. However, this was not the case with Silly Putty.

A General Electric engineer working on the synthetic rubber mixed boric acid and silicone oil, and came up with something that didn't work, but nevertheless had some unusual properties. When he dropped it, the material bounced higher than from where it had been released. It was impervious to rot. It was also soft and malleable. It could even be stretched many times its length without breaking. Finally, it could receive the image of any printed material that was pressed into it. The only trouble was, though it had all of those properties, there was one thing it was not. It was not a suitable substitute for the rubber coming from plants on islands now under enemy control.

A few years later, a man named Peter Hodgson attended a party at which this strange material was the entertainment. He witnessed adults playing with and enjoying the product for its properties. Hodgson looked into where the product had originated and who owned the rights. General Electric sold Hodgson the rights, and Hodgson named it Silly Putty. It became world famous and made Hodgson a fortune.[3]

Supply-side innovation, then, is based primarily on unexpected results, as it was with Silly Putty. But it's what you do with those unexpected results that makes the difference; it's what gets you the promotion, the fame, and the fortune. Because of the focused demands of the war and the lack of rigorous logical analysis after the war, no successful innovation resulted from this discovery at GE. I don't mean that GE should have gone into the toy business; I only mean that GE could have found a way to use this unexpected innovation. Peter Hodgson was just a guest at a party, but he grasped its potential and created the new product. He didn't go to the party to witness a demonstration of this product's capabilities, or even go knowing that the product existed. He did not decide instantly that he would create a profitable and internationally famous toy. But over time he used analysis and investigation, which ultimately resulted in the successful innovation and accomplished exactly that. Note: Some potential supply-side innovations are rejected outright by those with the capability of exploiting them—something you should be particularly careful not to do.

Whether your organization is responsible for sales, human resources, finance, or another facet of business, has it ever made this kind of error? All sorts of unexpected results crop up in business, and they are commonly ignored or rejected outright, instead of being exploited as supply-side innovations.

Example: The Master of Supply-Side Innovation

Entrepreneur E. Joseph "Joe" Cossman, whom I have mentioned several times elsewhere in this book, built his fortune through innovation, almost entirely through supply-side innovation. Consider the Cossman ant farm. No one had ever heard of an ant farm until Cossman came along, yet the product had existed since the turn of the twentieth century. Essentially an ant cage made of wood and glass, the ant farm came with instructions on how to select the soil and get the ants to build a colony, the activity of which could then be observed through the glass. Of course, because it was made of glass, the cage represented a potential danger to children. Adults, mostly teachers, were advised to supervise children while they observed the ants at work. It was not considered a toy—rather, more of an educational tool. And only a few thousand of these ant cages were sold every year. Cossman looked at this educational tool and realized that construction materials had changed dramatically since the 1890s. If the colony's cage could be constructed of clear plastic, the dangers of unsupervised observation by children would be eliminated. Then, the ant colony would no longer be just an educational tool but also an educational toy that every child could own and enjoy at home. Substituting new plastic materials for the old wood and glass structures constituted innovation based on capability, and the unexpected results were based on this substitution. Cossman innovated and did the following as well to enhance its appeal:

- Renamed the product an "ant farm"

- Lowered the price based on using cheaper plastic materials and simpler manufacturing methods

- Provided a "stock certificate" with each unit sold, which would be sent to Cossman, who in return would guarantee the live delivery of twenty-five ants to start the farm

- Repositioned the product as a toy and sought new distribution channels

The results of this innovation were nothing short of spectacular. Cossman sold over 1 million ant farms, which propelled him into national fame. He even sold one ant farm to the White House for Caroline Kennedy.

But here's another example of Cossman's use of supply-side innovation. A company that was manufacturing diving equipment decided to make a diving toy. They connected a human figure in a diving helmet to a plastic bulb with a hose. The figure was weighted, and it sank when placed in a tub of water. A child could squeeze the plastic bulb, which would send air into the diving helmet, and the figure would rise to the surface. The problem was that plastic was the wrong material for the bulb. After only about ten squeezes, the bulb would crack and that would ruin the toy. Cossman bought the rights to the toy and its manufacturing machinery for a few hundred dollars.

Many people would simply have replaced the plastic bulb with a rubber bulb, and that would be it. But Cossman figured that the toy already had acquired a bad name. So he asked a chemistry professor at the local university if there was a harmless chemical he could use to make the figure move under water. "Sure," the professor replied, "baking soda pellets."

Cossman threw away the diving helmet, hose, and bulb; he added rubber flippers to the diving figure's feet, and where the hose had been attached, he inserted a baking powder pellet. His new product "swam" realistically underwater, and so he called it "Flippy, the Frogman." Cossman sold several hundred thousand Flippies. But then he noted some unexpected results: The frogman figure moving underwater also attracted fish. Presto, he had another product that he sold all over the world, called "Fisherman Joe's Fishing Lure."

Innovation Tactics

To develop areas where innovation can create maximum opportunities, Drucker recommended three questions for the would-be innovator to ask:[4]

1. What is lacking to make effective what is already possible?

2. What one small step would transform your economic results?

3. What small change would alter the capacity of the whole of your resources?

Can you apply supply-side innovation to your marketing or other duties? There's a fortune to be made if you can.

PART FOUR

4

Organization

CHAPTER THIRTY-TWO

The Purpose of Your Business Is Not to Make a Profit

Peter Drucker said and wrote a lot of things that on the surface sound absolutely outlandish. Perhaps this is what made him so "eminently quotable." That was all the more so when his seemingly ridiculous claim turned out to be true. Such was the case when he said one day that the purpose of a business was *not* to make a profit! Oh, come on, Peter—get real! If the purpose of a business is *not* to make a profit, then what is it? Everyone knows the very basic "fact" that the purpose of any business is to make money. That is to say, to make a profit. This "fact" leads to a corollary: that the goal of any business is to make as much profit as possible. That is, profit maximization.

Now, if you accept the principle that making a profit is, in fact, a business's purpose, the second half just follows naturally. Profit maximization might even seem like a worthy objective to many. For instance, it was the creed of Michael Douglas's character Gordon Gekko in the 1987 movie *Wall Street*, so well stated as "Greed is good." Even today, many in business "know" that greed, or profit maximization, is the correct prescription for business success, even if it doesn't seem to be "good" from a moral perspective.

As mentioned earlier, Drucker maintained that "whatever everyone knows is usually wrong," and certainly Hollywood films are not excepted. He emphasized, first, that profit is not the purpose of business, and following that, he maintained that the concept of profit maximization was not only meaningless but also dangerous.[1]

Why the Myth of Profit Maximization Is a Fallacy

Many economists consider profit maximization a basic theorem. But Drucker said if you strip this theorem down to its fundamental principle, it is simply another way of saying that a business should buy low and sell high. That's pretty basic, right? However, he noted that this simple description doesn't begin to explain the success or failure of a business—any business.

For example, a local retailer may have been buying low and selling high. If that's all that you know, you don't know enough to claim that the business is a success (or a failure). Look at all the businesses that closed during the recession. Weren't all of them buying low and selling high, or at least attempting to do so? Consider the difficulties faced by many businesses struggling today to avoid joining the many failures that have already occurred. So, it is clear that buying low and selling high explains very little about why these businesses have failed, just as that idea explains very little about those who are successful, or those who are accelerating their success despite the obstacles they face.

Profit maximization seems to imply that you might save a business from failure by simply raising prices and creating a greater differential between revenue and cost—that is, that you maintain (or increase) the profit margin. In point of fact, as costs to businesses rise, be they gasoline, materials, or anything else, raising prices is the immediate and simplistic response that many businesses make. Yet these businesses still fail or succeed, independent of their act of raising prices. Thus, profit maximization by itself is absolutely not the determining factor for success or failure.

Not so long ago I was told that a local restaurant failed owing to the rising cost of fresh produce. Yet other restaurants in the same general area, serving the same target market, did not fail. Some are thriving and even increasing their sales, even though the cost of produce rose for all equally.[2] Clearly, just creating a certain level of profit isn't the overriding factor.

But What About the Profit Motive?

The idea of profit motive was also fair game for Drucker's genius. The profit motive is yet another basic economic concept. On the face of it, there is little to question. A typical definition is: "The intent to achieve monetary gain in a transaction or material endeavor. Profit motive can also be construed as the underlying reason why a taxpayer or company participates in business activities of any kind."[3] Many economists take the macro view that in order to maximize an economy's growth, one must also maximize profits.[4]

But Drucker called the profit motive into question. He claimed that there has never been any evidence for such a motive, and that the theory was invented by classical economists to explain a reality that their theory of economic equilibrium could not fathom. Let's consider an example.

There is a good deal of volunteerism done, in which individuals—some quite highly paid in other roles, others not—work long, hard hours for the common good. They work in religious and community groups doing a variety of socially beneficial activities. Many don't get paid a penny for their efforts. Many other talented individuals knowingly choose occupations that are less financially rewarding so as to follow a personal interest or calling to help others. Drucker challenged the view that sky-high corporate salaries were necessary to attract quality personnel—that these people "would not work for less" owing to the *profit motive*. Yet, there are many top jobs that attract high-quality individuals but offer them extremely low pay.

For example, an organization that tracks corporate salaries listed top-rated charity organizations at which, even today, the CEOs earn annual salaries of only $21,000 to $58,000.[5] Moreover, a top-ranked military commander—a four-star general, who may be responsible for the welfare and lives of from several hundred thousand to more than a million subordinates, responsible for millions of dollars worth of equipment, and accountable for outcomes of extreme importance—earns the relatively low compensation of about $200,000 a year.

From this we can conclude that while the prospect of profit can be motivating, it need not be the *primary* motivator; hence, the notion of maximizing profit as the goal for a business, or the life purpose of an individual, is at best overstated.

Now, don't get the idea that the need for profitability is a waste of time or is immoral, however. Of course, there are "bad people" in business—all businesses—and there always will be. But this reality causes some people to question the basic principles of capitalism and to wonder whether any profit is necessary at all. As a result, the profit motive is viewed as worse than irrelevant: It does harm because it creates hostility toward earning a profit—something Drucker called "the most dangerous disease of an industrial society."

Drucker felt that this "disease" ends up causing some of the worst mistakes of public policy and promotes the notion that there is an inherent contradiction between profits and an organization's making a social contribution. As he noted, a company can only make a social contribution *if* it is profitable.

Some otherwise smart people in the nonprofit sector, in perhaps the epitome of ignorance, say, "I don't make a profit. Why should a business?" But Drucker proved that profitability—far from being a myth, immoral, or unnecessary—is *crucial* for the success of both individual businesses and society in general. Moreover, he considered profit (as opposed to profit maximization) even more important for society than for an individual business. However, profit is not the purpose of a business.

What Is the Purpose of a Business?

There is only one valid purpose for a business: to create a customer. As Drucker wrote, "The customer is the foundation of a business and keeps it in existence. He alone gives employment. To supply the wants and needs of a consumer, society entrusts wealth-producing resources to the business enterprise."[6] In other words, society gives the business the means to achieve its purpose (gain a customer), in return for supplying the needs and wants of society's consumers. That sounds reasonable. But why is profit maximization not at least a goal of business?

Profits Pay for Innovation

Profit and profitability are absolute requirements. That's why even nonprofit corporations must strive mightily for "profitability." The dean of a major business school recently confided to me that his school had been running in the red for several years. "Pretty good recommendation for a school of management, right?" he asked me sardonically. However, to return to Drucker, profit is not the basic purpose of a business. Instead, profitability is an essential ingredient of business, and is best spoken of in terms of optimal, rather than maximum, size.

The primary test of any business is not its maximization of profit, but the achievement of sufficient profit to allow for the risks of the financial activity, and to avoid any catastrophic loss leading to failure. Only through an *optimal* profit might a business achieve the success that will benefit both the business and society. So, profit is necessary, but it is not the purpose of business.

What was Drucker's logic? That profit is like oxygen for the human body. Oxygen ensures that the body lives, survives, and grows. Without oxygen, the body withers and dies, just as a business does without profit. And just as the body demands oxygen, so does a business demand profit, whether that business is legally incorporated as for-profit or is nonprofit. Both forms of business need profit to survive.

Why do both types of business need profit? Because the profit goes to support the two basic functions of any business: marketing and innovation. According to Drucker, these functions are needed to create action. Only a business action can create a customer, and that means innovation, advertising, salesmanship, strategy, customer service, quality—you name it. These business actions cost money, which comes from the difference between buying low and selling high.

Pure Profit Leads to Failure

As stated earlier, it is *optimal* profit that is required, just as the body needs the right amount of oxygen to survive. Too much oxygen can cause damage to cell membranes, the collapse of the alveoli in the lungs, retinal detachment, and seizures, and eventually death. Similarly, too much profit—that is, profit maximization without consideration of other elements in the business's equation—can cause business problems.

If the focus of the business is solely on profit maximization, the customer may be ignored or given secondary consideration. This, in turn, can lead to poor management decisions that result in cutting corners on safety, service, or product performance. Additionally, if profit maximization drives the company's purpose, the competition that maintains a different focus—to win markets by providing greater value or charging less—will move in. Recently we have seen many industries err in this way. In truth, these bad decisions as a result of profit maximization—what might be termed organizational toxicity—can and do occur in all industries, and the result is the same as too much oxygen for the body. The business may die.

If profit maximization drives the company purpose, it can allow competition with a different focus to win markets by providing greater value or charging less. Profit maximization can cause organizational toxicity in the same way that oxygen toxicity can damage the body.

The Drucker Message

What has this to do with you or me? Well, regardless of your type of organization, and whether it operates for profit or not for profit, Drucker's truth holds. If you want your organization to be successful, you have to see profit as essential to support innovation and marketing actions, and view profit maximization as bad for society as well as hazardous to your organization's health.

CHAPTER THIRTY-THREE

Social Responsibility
Is a Win-Win

Some years ago a publication in Japan asked if I could do a lengthy piece on Peter Drucker's view of the social responsibility of business. This is not always a popular topic among corporate leaders. Let's just say it's not number one on their list. They've got other things to worry about: competition, government regulations, advancing technology, management-worker relations, marketing, innovation, and a lot more. It's not just that they view putting time and resources into social issues as a cost, but they also see it as a distraction from their primary responsibilities.

Drucker on Social Responsibility

Drucker believed that considerations for workers in and outside of the workplace were the responsibility of corporate leaders just as much as the profits, survival, and growth of their businesses or organizations. Social responsibilities were an integral part of doing business. He didn't hide those thoughts under a bush. Today, some would call Drucker a pioneer in the area of business social responsibility, although he probably would have denied this.

Drucker liked to point to the early spirit of responsibility shown by two very wealthy Americans of the nineteenth and twentieth centuries. One was an immigrant to the United States, as was Drucker. Andrew Carnegie, the son of a handloom weaver in Dumferline, Scotland, came to America with nothing and became one of the wealthiest men in U.S. history. Carnegie started working on railroads, but made his money as a steel tycoon. The American-born Julius Rosenwald was the son of Jewish immigrants from Germany who were engaged in what today is known as "the rag business." Rosenwald started a clothing manufacturing company and eventually became part owner of Sears, Roebuck and Company. He initiated the growth that turned the store into a worldwide colossus.

Both men gave fortunes away to help better society. Peter Drucker singled them out as early examples of how men who made their wealth in society returned the money to society, even as they built their fortunes and their businesses. Among the better known of this type of individual today is Bill Gates. However, being socially responsible means far more than simply giving money away.

Here are five of Drucker's major thoughts regarding what a corporation must do to be socially responsible:

1. Don't leave it to government.

2. The corporate mission comes first.

3. There is an unlimited liability clause.

4. There are unique ethics of social responsibility.

5. There are opportunities for competitive advantage inherent in being socially responsible.

Let's take each, in turn.

Don't Leave It to Government

Drucker found increasing disenchantment with government's ability to successfully initiate or successfully implement social programs. For example, although government coordinates 4-H Club activities in the United States today, it was a businessman, Julius Rosenwald, who originally initiated and developed this concept. It was only after Rosenwald was successful that government stepped in.

Drucker said, "There is now no developed country—whether free enterprise or communist—in which people still expect government programs to succeed."[1] He gave a number of reasons for the increasing failure of government to assume responsibilities for social problems or to be successful in achieving worthwhile results. However, his overriding reason was that government, by necessity, served too many constituencies. This made it extremely difficult, if not impossible, to set specific goals and objectives, since powerful constituencies have different goals and different values. Frequently, these goals and objectives are mutually exclusive. Yet without agreed goals and objectives, social programs are doomed from the start. Drucker's point was that when corporations see something that needs doing, they should just go ahead and do it.

The Corporate Mission Comes First

If the effort to achieve a positive benefit results in harm to the organization initiating it, this is not socially responsible action, regardless of the good intentions. According to Drucker, the organization's first responsibility must always be to its own mission, regardless of other factors. The first "social responsibility" of a business is to make a profit sufficient to cover its operational costs in the future. If the business fails in its attempt to fulfill a particular social responsibility—possibly because of misallocation of time, resources, or personnel—not only does that prevent it from solving that social problem but it fails society in not meeting its mission and in wasting society's resources.

This point goes back to Drucker's primary purpose of a business: to create a *customer*, not to create a profit. Customers enable the business to be profitable, while the business fills society's needs and wants. If the organization fails in its primary mission, there is no need for it and it goes out of existence. So if this basic social responsibility of fulfilling the organization's purpose is not met, no other social responsibility can be met, either.[2]

Unfortunately, advocates for various causes frequently pressure organizations to resolve social issues that are totally outside the organization's area of expertise or its ability to comply. And the actions desired by these groups would hurt the organizations—hence, society as well. Failing to take the action desired, these organizations are sometimes called "greedy" or "unethical." Drucker would counter that argument by noting that the pressure groups themselves are greedy or unethical, rather than the businesses that refuse to comply.

While nongovernmental organizations must assume responsibilities for solving some social problems, they must, above all, do nothing that impedes their own capacity to fulfill their obligations, which are the rationale for their existence.

Beware the Unlimited Liability Clause

Good intentions of themselves are not necessarily socially responsible, according to Drucker. Moreover, through failure to think through the potential outcomes, many organizations take actions to improve a social condition, only to create significant and unintended negative impacts.

With an "unlimited liability clause" imposed by society, the organization taking the action assumes responsibility for the outcome, no matter what—and not just for the present, but also into the future. Most social advocates, as well as general consumers, view high prices as a social problem that must be addressed. Sam Walton recognized this and built his company, Walmart, into the world's largest retailer by selling quality goods at reduced prices. Walton initiated the cost-saving practices and established a new focus on low pricing, which benefited all consumers. Unfortunately, for Walmart, there were unintended results for which it had to be held accountable.

The same strategies that brought profit, success, and cheers from consumers earlier on also brought legal problems, governmental interference, and bad press later on. For example, Walmart was accused of forcing out smaller, local businesses that could not compete with Walmart's low prices. Moreover, Walmart kept its prices down partly by closely controlling and limiting the pay and benefits of its employees. Additionally, suppliers who were obligated to deal with the colossal buyer that Walmart had become accused the company of squeezing them into bankruptcy. Other studies claimed that Walmart's buying practices had forced manufacturing jobs overseas. Thus, to some, Walmart went from corporate "Good Guy" to corporate "Bad Actor." Yet Walmart had changed nothing.

Drucker taught that the impacts of decisions are inevitable. So, the first step toward being socially responsible is to minimize the bad impacts. Be careful when "doing good," for there is an "unlimited liability clause" to which—like it or not—corporations are held accountable for their actions, both in the present and into the future.

The Unique Ethics of Social Responsibility

Drucker struggled with the ethics of social responsibility. He did not find a solution that would cover all contingencies. He did feel that several basic Confucian concepts provided general guidelines that could be applied toward determining the ethics of social responsibility. He also believed that one general guideline applied to social responsibility as well: *Primum non nocere*, or "First, do no harm."[3]

Opportunities for Competitive Advantage in Social Responsibility

Today, social responsibility is the "in thing." Many corporations have entire departments with the purpose of encouraging social responsibility. They look at company actions that might be causing negative reactions, uncover opportunities for good, and develop and run socially responsible programs. It is easy to forget that this was not always so.

Even Alfred P. Sloan, General Motors' legendary CEO, claimed that social responsibility was not the concern of business and that the two should remain completely and forever separate. In one of his rare disagreements with Sloan's management precepts, Drucker proclaimed that fulfilling social responsibility was not only a duty but could also result in competitive advantage for a company, far beyond mere good public relations with the general public or its customers.

For instance, Julius Rosenwald became first vice president and treasurer, and then president, of an ailing, unprofitable Sears, Roebuck and Company in 1895. Under his leadership, sales increased an astounding 700 percent. While becoming a wealthy man, Rosenwald invested a lot of money during his lifetime for the betterment of society. This investment included $70 million for schools, colleges, and universities. To some, $70 million is peanuts, but in today's dollars this is equivalent to almost $2 billion.

You hear a lot about the Tuskegee Airmen today. These were the first African-American pilots to enter combat during World War II. They trained at Tuskegee Institute, in Alabama. In 1912, when prejudice was more prevalent than equal opportunity for minorities, Rosenwald donated the money to found this famous African-American agricultural school. In short, while Rosenwald implemented many socially responsible policies because it was the right thing to do, he also saw to it that the welfare of his company was based on the knowledge, skill, and well-being of the company's primary customers. In those days, this was American farmers. Rosenwald put a lot of money into agriculture, even though he was a city boy who didn't know a thing about farming. Intended or not, Rosenwald's social responsibility served a dual purpose: It not only helped people, it also built Sears Roebuck's customer base and helped develop its market. Within ten years, the company went from near bankruptcy to being the largest merchant in the world and one of America's most profitable and fastest-growing companies.[4] Social responsibility is, indeed, a major competitive advantage!

Social Responsibility Takes Many Forms

IBM's original approach to eliminating discrimination was simply to ignore the cultural, racial, and other differences among its worldwide workforce of more than 150,000 employees. When Lou Gerstner became CEO in 1993, he dropped this concept and initiated a diversity task force with a different approach and a different objective. The new objective was to uncover and understand the differences among the groups making up the IBM workforce and the markets they served. Then the task force was to use what was learned to find ways to appeal to a broader set of employees and customers.

This strategy worked. Understanding and using its corporate diversity became a major competitive advantage for IBM. As a result of Gerstner's initiative, the number of female executives in the company grew by 370 percent and the number of ethnic minority executives increased by 233 percent. All of this had a major effect on bottom-line profits. It led to efforts to develop a broader client base among businesses owned by women, Asians, African Americans, Hispanics, senior citizens, and Native Americans. This, in turn, resulted in a dramatic growth in revenue in the company's small- and medium-size business sales, from an earlier $10 million to hundreds of millions of dollars in just five years.[5]

Those who follow Drucker's ideas of social responsibility are not guaranteed success, but the contributions to the organizations of which they are members and to society can be of immense benefit. Somehow there is always significant value in just doing the right thing, which is even more important than any advantage that might accrue to those who perform acts of social responsibility. I think Peter would agree with this sentiment.

CHAPTER THIRTY-FOUR

There Are Only Two Organizational Functions

It's been sixty years since Drucker first wrote, "Because the purpose of business is to create a customer, the business enterprise has two—and only two—basic functions: marketing and innovation. Marketing and innovation produce results; all the rest are costs."[1]

Was he being overly simplistic? Was he mistaken? Was he denying the wisdom of pundits who for years had been saying that a business exists to make a profit, that its duty or responsibility was to its stockholders, customers, employees, and/or society? Or, was he just trying to make a point? Moreover, what has this got to do with you if you are a professional or first-line supervisor in an organization?

In much of what Drucker wrote, his concepts aren't limited to big business or higher management levels. They can and *should* be applied to small businesses, start-ups, governments, nonprofit organizations, and individual professionals, in whatever the line of work. Perhaps this isn't obvious because sometimes Drucker's ideas aren't immediately obvious. They require us to think through his ideas and apply them to ourselves.

Maybe that is one reason he used only a single "textbook" in several of his courses. It was not really a textbook in the true sense. It was his seminal work: *Management, Tasks, Responsibilities, Practices.*[2] The book had over 800 pages, but that's not unusual for management texts. The "Drucker difference" in this case was how he used the book to supplement his lectures.

Many professors divide an 800-page textbook into its parts to correspond with the classes in the term, so that by the end of the course the students have gone through the entire book. But Drucker said that it was impossible to master the contents of an 800-page book in one course. So his students were responsible only for a limited number of chapters. Moreover, if students took another Drucker course, they simply got familiar with a different set of chapters from the same book.

Drucker, No Nostradamus

Understanding Drucker is sometimes not too different from trying to comprehend the predictions of early astrologers, such as the sixteenth-century Italian Nostradamus. The problem with reading Nostradamus's predictions today is that no matter how amazingly accurate they seemed to be in their time, they are difficult to interpret now. Detractors point out that since these ancients are viewed with hindsight, people tend to analyze their predictions so as to confirm their accuracy. This is not true of Drucker, however.

Among his economic and business predictions, Drucker proves to have been right. He foresaw the rise of the healthcare industry and the future of online executive education. Also, fifty years ago he warned us of the terrible price society would pay as a result of the greed of both management and labor—consequences that we feel today. Although he had hoped to become a professor at the University of Cologne, Peter Drucker escaped Germany only days after Hitler took power. He knew what Hitler was about, and there certainly is little doubt about the accuracy of Drucker's predictions in this case.

Nevertheless, there is still sometimes a mysterious touch of Nostradamus in Drucker's observations and in trying to apply his advice to business operations today. Years ago, a reviewer noted of Drucker's writings, "It's not that Drucker isn't explicit; he is very explicit in everything he writes. The problem is, Drucker frequently tells us what to do, but not how to do it."

The Essential Nature of Innovation

As noted above, Drucker wrote that innovation and marketing are the two basic functions of any business. *Innovation* refers to the introduction of something new and better. He confirmed this in his assertion that if a business continued to do what made it successful in the past, it would eventually fail. Though not obvious, that point applies to any organization today. It seems logical that if a company has been successful, it should keep doing what has made it successful, with the expectation that it will continue to do so. Yet, as usual, Drucker was right.

Of course, some examples of this are so evident that one wonders how anyone can miss the point. Henry Ford made millions of dollars with his Model T, "the car of the century." Yet this wonderfully successful vehicle also caused Ford to lose a good part of its market to General Motors for forty years as the Model T went through its life cycle. As pointed out in Chapter 23, this happened because Henry Ford refused to accept that potential customers were prepared to pay more for a variety of options. Ford stubbornly would not provide these options because, blinded by past success, he was convinced that allowing even just the paint color to deviate from basic black would be an unnecessary concession to a temporary aberration and would befoul the legacy of his car's success. This sort of thing happens all the time.

Example: Burma-Shave and Its Highway Signs

Innovation can be many things, but its success does not go on forever. Remember those roadside Burma-Shave signs? You could not escape them years ago. It all started with a failing company that manufactured a brushless shaving cream, the ingredients of which supposedly originated in the Malay Peninsula and Burma. Its marketing innovation was novel, exciting, timely, and wildly successful.

This was the early 1920s, and America had fallen in love with the automobile—and not only Ford's Model T. By the millions, Americans took to the highways. Fun, yes, but also a little boring. Cars could travel at only a relatively modest speed in those days. So, the Burma-Shave people put small signs at intervals along the road, spacing out the short messages so they could be read easily. Space for the signs was rented from farmers at low cost. Americans were soon reading little sayings, such as:

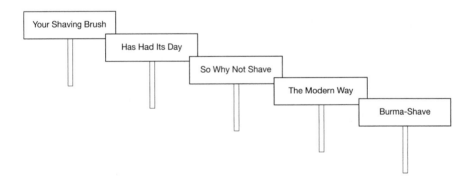

Soon there were 7,000 such jingles lining America's highways, and Burma-Shave sales soared such that the company's product became the number two choice for shaving cream. Burma-Shave stood out in American marketing and advertising endeavors. It was different from anything else and it had its own personality. It became part of the national culture. People talked about the signs, they were mentioned in the entertainment media, and the lyrics even began to include public-service messages, such as:

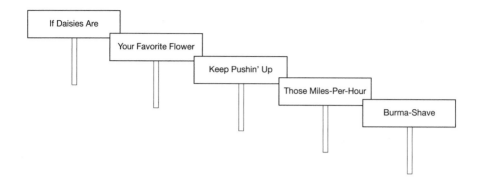

If Daisies Are

Your Favorite Flower

Keep Pushin' Up

Those Miles-Per-Hour

Burma-Shave

But in 1963 the signs suddenly disappeared. What had happened? It was the same old story. The signs were originally highly successful, so the company continued the same campaign—the campaign never changed. Automobiles did—they traveled a lot faster. Billboards changed, too—they got bigger and more costly. The signs drew competition. Suddenly this successful innovation was no longer a novelty. More important, the signs no longer attracted customers.[3,4,5]

Innovation Required!

In my years of consulting for local small businesses, I was amazed at the numbers of businesses whose owners went into business without understanding that a mere desire to open a retail store, laundry, restaurant, or barbershop did not guarantee customers. A large number of them hadn't considered the question of why a prospect should buy from them rather than from an established enterprise already serving the area. Innovation, as well as marketing, was always needed.

Drucker Views Marketing

Drucker's second basic function of business is *marketing*. Why is marketing a basic function? The answer is bound up in the terms *selling* and *marketing*. Most people think that marketing and selling are pretty much the same, but they are mistaken. Drucker knew that they are not the same, and he was one of the first to write about this. Moreover, he taught that good selling could actually be adversarial to good marketing.

How can this be? Remember that an important aspect of selling is to persuade a prospect to buy something that you have. On the other hand, marketing involves telling a prospect what you have that he or she wants. Making decisions on where to invest your time, money, and effort is part of marketing. So, marketing is much broader and more strategic than selling.

Drucker liked to say that if marketing were done perfectly, selling would be unnecessary. Of course, it's not unnecessary; selling is absolutely necessary. However, good selling of a product or service you shouldn't be selling is a waste of time, money, and effort; you need to move on and seek something more valued by your prospect. Then you can sell easier, at lower cost, and in greater quantities than you would have sold that other product or service. With this perspective, good selling may indeed be the enemy of good marketing.

Innovation and Marketing Apply to You

As with other Drucker insights, this insight about innovation and marketing applies to you, as an individual, as well as to any business with which you might be associated. If you are doing a competent job and are successful as an HR professional or a nuclear scientist, you had better think about innovating, especially when the economy is tough. Innovation and marketing are the ingredients of business success, and they are the essentials of personal success as well. Drucker was right again.

CHAPTER THIRTY-FIVE

Ignorance Is Good

When Peter Drucker would begin classroom instruction for a course, he sometimes would make a seemingly outlandish statement to make a point. On one occasion, he began to reminisce about his work with various corporations, both here and in Japan. He described how often very simple things an outsider might do could have a major impact on the company. This was because the people involved were generally too close to the problems and assumed too much based on their past experiences, which they incorrectly thought were identical to the present situation. An outsider, however, would question aspects of business that a practicing manager frequently missed. Asked the secret of his success in these endeavors, Drucker responded, "There is no secret. You just need to ask the right questions."

Unexpectedly, some of the students asked:

"How do you know the right questions to ask?"

"Aren't your questions based on your knowledge of the industries in which you consult?"

"What about when first starting out, with no experience; how did you have the knowledge and expertise to do this when you began and had little experience?"

Drucker responded, "I never ask these questions or approach these assignments based on my knowledge and experience. It is exactly the opposite. I do not use my knowledge and experience at all. I bring only my ignorance to the situation. Ignorance is the most important component for approaching any problem in any industry."

The students were more excited than satisfied with this answer, but Peter waved them off. "Ignorance is not such a bad thing if one knows how to use it," he continued, "and all managers must learn how to do this. You must frequently approach problems with your ignorance; not what you think you know, because not infrequently, what you think you know is wrong."

Ignorance Has Value in Problem Solving

Drucker immediately launched into a story to prove his point. And his stories covered the wide range of his reading and thinking. One minute he was talking about Japanese culture, the next moment Jewish mysticism or warfare. The point is that since ignorance was something I recognized I had in abundance, Drucker's admonition that there was value in ignorance inspired me to seek a simple methodology to analyze problems. Although I found many methods that meet this criterion, the four-step one described here is my favorite and the one that I have used the most.

1. Define the Problem

You can't get "there" until you know where "there" is. That's not one of Peter Drucker's injunctions; it's one of mine. That's my way of emphasizing that, in order to solve any problem, you've first got to understand exactly what the problem is. You can see why Drucker's instruction to begin with *ignorance* is so important. If the problem has been defined incorrectly, based on past knowledge, you are not going to arrive at the best solution.

For example, early in WWII, the British were losing a lot of ships to German submarines. The British had built many of their ships in the prewar days. They followed plans based on their prior knowledge, experience, and skilled shipbuilding labor force so as to reduce the construction time for one of these ships to slightly less than a year. However, they continued to lose ships to the German submarines, and because their labor force was fully engaged in the war effort, they were losing ships faster than they could build them. Finally, the British turned the whole thing over to the United States, which was still at peace and had the manpower, if not the shipbuilding expertise, to get the job done. The British hoped that their Yankee partners could turn out the needed ships in two years.

If only the problem had been defined as "How can we build ships the British way without the same human and physical resources?" Then, the answer would have been "We can't." Industrialist Henry Kaiser, with almost no experience in shipbuilding or a labor force skilled at shipbuilding, was the first to take on the task in the United States. If Kaiser's ignorance hadn't been brought to the problem, so that the question was rephrased, Kaiser and other potential U.S. emergency shipbuilders might still be working on finding the solution—or long since decided that it couldn't be done. With 1940s technology, that problem just couldn't have been solved. So Kaiser abandoned the British plan, redefined the problem, and used what he had to produce the ships.

2. Determine Relevant Factors

Kaiser needed to gather additional data. He knew what he didn't have; he needed to know what resources he did have. After looking into this, he determined that he could build these ships cheaper and faster.

3. Consider Alternative Courses of Action

Kaiser had to decide on alternatives to solve the problem. One option might be to develop new tactics. Maybe he could start a worldwide search for expert shipbuilders in neutral countries and offer them high wages. Maybe he could design new metal-cutting machinery and produce it quickly using his methods. It is possible he did consider these or other options.

In any case, Kaiser took an enormous risk with his solution. He had invested millions of dollars in it before he even built his first ship. Many of the methods he used had never been employed previously, and some were extremely innovative, to say the least. For example, it was reported that because it took years and extensive training to enable novice fitters to tightrope across the high structures of the ship as it was completed, Kaiser hired ballet dancers to work as fitters.

The British had expert workers with general, but in-depth shipbuilding knowledge. Since he didn't have such workers, Kaiser asked himself how he could proceed and came up with a unique solution. Based on his ignorance of shipbuilding, Kaiser redesigned the assembly process using prefabricated parts, so that no worker had to know more than a small part of the job. This method made his workers much easier to train, in less time—weeks instead of years.

Then, Kaiser introduced American assembly-line techniques. The British knew that for close tolerances in high-quality ships, heavy machinery was needed to cut metal accurately. Kaiser didn't know this—and anyway, he didn't have the heavy machinery. Again, he asked himself a question: "How do I cut the metal?" And again, he came up with a solution. He told his workers to cut the metal using oxyacetylene torches, something the British had not been doing. Amazingly, this turned out to be a cheaper and faster method than the traditional British one. In his ignorance, Kaiser replaced riveting with welding, also cheaper and faster. He called his products "Liberty Ships."[1]

4. Analysis, Conclusions, and Decision

During the analysis phase, a manager essentially compares the relative importance of each of the existing alternatives along with their advantages and disadvantages. Some alternatives have few disadvantages, but they have no great advantage, either. In any case, the manager needs to think through the situation and document that thinking. This ensures that there's an effective explanation for the decision making.

Henry Kaiser undoubtedly went through this process in detail when explaining what he wanted to do to his managers, workers, and board of directors. He would have left nothing out, concluding that despite the risks the best way to achieve the desired results was to implement the building of the British ships in the way he had outlined.

What were Kaiser's results? Well, he never did build a ship in the slightly less than one-year time period that the British method had managed with their skilled workers. No, sir! His first ships were completed in about a month. Then, they got the production time down to a couple weeks. And if that weren't enough, for publicity purposes, they constructed one Liberty Ship in just four-and-a-half days!

The Role of Ignorance in Problem Solving

My conclusions regarding Drucker's lesson on ignorance and problem solving is that no one need fear being incapable of solving a problem, whether managerial or otherwise, because of ignorance. While a manager may lack specific knowledge, experience, or expertise at the beginning of the quest, this is not necessarily a bad thing. On the contrary, beginning with ignorance, and recognizing it for what it is, is possibly the best way to approach any problem.

I understand that one of Drucker's consulting clients complained that he never told them what to do—that he only asked questions. "That was a little disconcerting at first," reminisced the client. "However, we soon realized that our having to think through the answers to the questions he asked was causing us to come up with solutions that were making us a good deal of money."

CHAPTER THIRTY-SIX

What to Do When an Organization Faces a Crisis

Peter Drucker didn't predict economic or financial crises, or say what to do about them—at least after 1929. As I've mentioned elsewhere in this book, the last time he attempted to analyze and predict an economic situation was that year, when he claimed there would be continual economic expansion and good times in the coming decade. A few weeks later, the bottom fell out of the market, resulting in the Great Depression. To the best of my knowledge, he never again made any predictions having to do with the stock market.

Drucker's Infallible Predictions

Chapter 34 mentions Drucker's near infallibility in predicting major political, social, and business developments, and what to do about them. As noted, he foresaw the rise of Hitler at a time when practically every European political analyst had written him off as inconsequential.

Importantly, Drucker predicted the rise of the "knowledge worker," a term he created to describe the new worker who performed more with his mind than his body. He envisioned that the day of "carrot or stick" management as prime motivator would be over. He anticipated the rise of the healthcare industry; the tremendous expansion of executive education; the impact of technology on business and education, especially the Internet; and the major contribution that online education would make in the future.

For years he railed against the unreasonably high salaries paid to executives. He pointed out that in the United States the ratio of highest paid executive in a company to its lowest paid worker was the widest in the world, better than 300 to 1. Drucker said it shouldn't be more than 20 to 1. He was against golden parachutes. He warned that we would pay a terrible price for these gifts to retiring executives, and, of course, that is exactly what has happened.

Many of the things Drucker pointed to were controversial and difficult to swallow, perhaps all the more so because they were so accurate. If Drucker's wisdom had been applied in the past, it would have prevented crises in many companies, organizations, and countries. But consider this: What if a crisis occurs anyway?

Face the Difficult Facts and Take Action

A leader must expect positive results with new initiatives, or he'd never take the necessary risks; the alternative is to achieve little but mediocrity. However, when bad things happen, and a crisis is pending as a result, the negative facts need to be faced squarely and dealt with on that basis. Positive action needs to be taken.

Positive action means confronting the truth about a situation and immediately letting those affected know what has happened, as well as what actions can be taken. In almost every instance of *ultimate* failure, the problem could have been fixed, or at least the negative outcomes significantly mitigated, if the responsible individuals had faced the facts, taken positive action, and kept others informed.

Do What's Right

A good many of the problems we face in our current financial crisis are due to the actions of people who should have known better, but did not just do what's right. It may have started with a potential borrower who knows he can't afford a house, and maybe hasn't even saved the money for a down payment. You recall the advertisements: NO MONEY DOWN. This borrower justified the loan in thinking that housing prices would keep going up—forever. And the mortgage broker didn't much care, since he wasn't making the loan, anyway. He still got his commission, so he might not have checked that potential borrower as closely as he should have. In any case, what was the difference, since housing prices would always go up? And the bank made the loan, since it would eventually pass it on to an investment firm for bundling as investment securities sold on Wall Street. And anyway, didn't the government say that every American should be able to afford his or her own home, and had loosened the restrictions on borrowing to permit this to happen?

Housing prices would always go up. That was what people all told themselves, at every level, to justify actions that they knew were wrong. Wall Street bankers could create an investment fund with all these mortgages, good and bad, and sell the fund to "sophisticated" institutional investors, insurance companies, and the like. Even if forewarned that some of these loans were marginal, they assumed that not all of the loans in a package would go bad. Wall Street, too, knew better, but the experts figured that real estate would always increase in value. In short, everybody involved at every level justified his or her actions on the basis of the belief that the value of housing would always increase. But just like any Ponzi scheme, the bubble eventually bursts and, when it does, there are severe consequences. This is an example of not doing the right thing.

It's too late to "walk the cat" back. So, now what? Doing what's right now won't automatically get the country out of a mess or save an individual homeowner or a bank or small business. But it will get us back on track, and it will help restore confidence in a system that has gone awry. Doing the right thing will also help with other crises that have not yet occurred. So, do what's right in your business dealings. That may not always be easy, but it will contribute toward getting things turned around.

Had Enron's Kenneth Lay admitted the situation when he realized what had been going on in his company, and had he taken true corrective action instead of telling the world everything was fine while dumping his own stock, the company and its employees would still have suffered, but they may have survived, and so might have he.

Share the Pain

Suppose you are in a position of responsibility, with supervision of subordinates. Drucker's lesson regarding crises is to share the pain. Consider another man named Ken. Ken Iverson was CEO of Nucor, a steel company, the third largest in the nation. It consistently racked up high profits even in a declining industry. Nucor's 7,000 employees were the best-paid workers in the steel business, yet they had the industry's lowest labor costs per ton of steel produced. Although Nucor was a Fortune 500 company, only twenty-four people were assigned to corporate headquarters, and there were only four layers of management, from the CEO to the frontline worker.

Then a major recession hit the steel industry. The total number of steelworkers dropped almost overnight industry-wide, by 50 percent. At Nucor, they had to cut production in half. However, Iverson didn't downsize anyone. Instead, he shared the pain. Iverson insisted that management take large pay cuts. The department heads took pay cuts of up to 40 percent. The company officers cut their salaries up to 60 percent. At a time when some Fortune 500 CEOs were taking home much more money, Iverson cut his own pay from $450,000 to $110,000—a salary cut of more than 75 percent. Nucor got through three years of industry-wide depression without laying off a single worker.

The Leader Is Always Responsible

Drucker emphasized that *leadership* was essential. In fact, in 1947, before people understood that there was a distinct difference between management and leadership, Drucker had declared that in an article in *Harper's* magazine: "Management is leadership," he wrote.[1]

This was about the importance of leadership. Toward the end of his career, Drucker wrote that leadership was a "marketing job." He said this partly because so much of being a good leader has to do with persuasion. Also, he pointed out that both concepts are so broad that they overlap significantly.

Consider the financial crisis that started late in 2008. The Bush administration got our attention about the crisis and President Bush immediately moved to introduce a solution, taking measures to stave off complete collapse. So far, so good. But bringing the problem to our attention and initiating action is only part of what constitutes leadership. As Drucker noted, a leader needs to do even more. No one explained satisfactorily what would happen if a $700 billion bailout wasn't immediately agreed to by Congress, or how it would work, or how the figure was arrived at, or even if other alternatives had been considered. A bailout of Wall Street firms was hardly attractive to most people, dealing with their immediate credit problems. It wasn't their fault. What difference would it make if "the fat cats" or "the greedy ones" paid for their errors? Let Wall Street bail itself out or fail, if that's how the chips fell.

In fact, with little effort made to explain or persuade the constituents, these voters across the country wrote their congressmen thirty to one *against* approving the bailout. Of course, the legislation was passed anyway. Was it the right thing to do? The wisdom of the bailout is still being debated. The point is that leadership and marketing, including precise goal setting and selling (persuasion), are always needed but never provided.

The Bush administration is not the only guilty party in its coping with this crisis. Certainly the Obama administration that followed has had plenty of opportunity to provide leadership through goal setting and persuasion. It also has dropped the ball in some cases, such as in explaining the expansion of healthcare. It is equally obvious in both administrations how much leadership is linked with other activities and how difficult it is to get things done, regardless of political party, popularity of the leader, or changing situations. Leadership is not easy, especially in a crisis. Nevertheless, it is the leader's responsibility, for better or worse.

Example: A General Takes Charge

I was always impressed by the actions of then Lieutenant General Bernard L. Montgomery, when he took charge of the British Eighth Army in Africa during World War II. Montgomery faced major problems. The Eighth Army had been defeated repeatedly by the German General Rommel and his Afrika Korps. After finally winning a victory, Montgomery's predecessor, General Auchinleck, had been persuaded to attack. Unfortunately, he had done so prematurely and had been defeated.

There was the possibility of an immediate counterattack by Rommel. The Eighth Army had made withdrawal after withdrawal. Orders were sent to prepare for yet another withdrawal; morale was at an all-time low. It was at this time that Montgomery was sent in. Here's what Montgomery did during his first day in charge:

- He canceled all previous orders about withdrawal.

- He declared that even in the event of enemy attack, there would be no withdrawal. The Eighth Army would fight on the ground they held. Or, in Montgomery's words, "If we couldn't stay there alive, we would stay there dead."

- He appointed a new chief of staff.

- He formed a new armored corps from "various bits and pieces."

- He changed the basic fighting units from brigade groups and ad hoc columns to full divisions. (Drucker called any reorganization "major surgery," so Montgomery had performed major surgery on his first day while his troops feared an enemy attack.)

- He initiated plans for an offensive, saying, "Our mandate is to destroy Rommel and his army, and it will be done as soon as we are ready."

Speaking later of the events of this first day being in charge, Montgomery said, "By the time I went to bed that night, I was tired. But I knew that we were on the way to success."[2] He was.

Sure, Montgomery faced different challenges, a different situation, and different authority to get others to do what he thought was necessary. But neither President Bush nor President Obama had to face the fact that whatever he did would cause immediate casualties, even death, based on his decision.

How Leaders Should Face a Crisis

Let's summarize Drucker's lessons about handling a crisis: No matter your level of work or management, the basic idea is to be a leader. A real leader does the things that lesser leaders refuse to do:

- They face the difficult facts and take action.

- They do the right thing.

- They share the pain.

- They take action.

Applying these leadership principles to your work will mark you as a real leader and help relieve the suffering in any crisis.

CHAPTER THIRTY-SEVEN

The Ultimate Requirement for Running a Good Organization

Ask management experts what the primary requirement is for running a good organization, and you'll get a variety of answers. Peter Drucker had only one answer: "Making the right people decisions is the ultimate means of controlling an organization well. Such decisions reveal how competent management is, what its values are, and whether it takes its job seriously."[1] People decisions start with staffing.

Staff for Strength

Unfortunately, staffing isn't easy, and there are some strong disagreements about how to make the right decisions. For example, you may be in an organization where the hiring philosophy is, "We want well-rounded individuals; we promote people who can do anything reasonably well and make few mistakes." To Drucker, these were the wrong answers. He said you should staff for strength to *accomplish* things, not to avoid mistakes.

This admonition stood out when I first read it because I knew how much Drucker admired the military and its way of doing things. Yet, the U.S. military, at least over the last half century or so, is definitely in the camp of the "well-rounded" individual and has tended to promote such people to the higher ranks. For example, a website on U.S. Air Force Academy admissions says, "Our investment in developing well-rounded leaders at the Academy pays untold dividends to our nation."[2]

Drucker, however, pointed out that many great leaders have had weaknesses that, according to the "well-rounded" view, should have kept them out of leadership roles. For example, Winston Churchill and Franklin D. Roosevelt drank to excess. General George Patton had a terrible temper. Ronald Reagan got bored easily and sometimes fell asleep during briefings. Even Jack Welch, legendary CEO of General Electric, a man who has been called the greatest business executive of the last century, mused once that maybe he was a little too emotional.

Here are Drucker's three prime rules for good staffing:[3]

1. Think through the requirements of the job.

2. Choose three or four candidates for the job rather than immediately settling on one.

3. Don't make the selection without discussing the choice with a number of knowledgeable colleagues.

Think Through the Requirements of the Job

A poorly designed job may be an impossible job that no one can do. What you get is work that is done poorly or not at all. In addition, a poorly designed job risks waste or, at best, the misallocation of scarce and valuable human resources.

To design a job properly, you need to thoroughly analyze the objectives and requirements of the job, deciding which few requirements are really crucial to that job's performance. A long list of requirements won't do it.

In a similar vein, you want to avoid a candidate who minimally meets all requirements of the job, but isn't particularly strong in the few critical areas that are essential. When Abraham Lincoln wanted to promote his most successful general, Ulysses S. Grant, to be general-in-chief of the Union forces during the Civil War, one of his cabinet officers warned that Lincoln should not expect too much from Grant because he was a hard drinker. Lincoln retorted, "Ask his brand so I can send a case to all my generals." Lincoln knew what was important to win the war.

Choose Multiple Candidates for a Job

Many promotions are made with only one or, at most, two candidates having been considered. According to Drucker, you should consider three or four candidates, all of whom meet the minimum qualifications of staffing for strength. This wisdom is frequently ignored, as hiring executives make assumptions about other candidates' suitability before measuring any of their qualifications against the prime job requirements.

In one organization, the staffing executive, who had been with the company for a year, wanted to appoint a particular manager from within the company to a senior position. He sent the recommendation forward to be approved by his boss. His boss asked to see the résumés of additional internal candidates for the job. So, the staffing executive used the old ploy of straw candidates. He selected three additional candidates for the position. He did not know the three well or think there was anything special about them; in fact, he chose them for that reason.

The staffing executive sent all four résumés to his boss. In addition to demonstrating questionable integrity in using this ploy, he made two major errors. First, he did not think through all the job requirements, which his boss had done. In addition, he relied on his personal knowledge and opinion of the candidates, without investigating other aspects of their work. That would have been bad enough, but he even failed to read the résumés he sent forward. He merely attached a strong letter of recommendation for his candidate.

What the staffing executive did not know is that one of those three additional candidates had been with the organization for many years and had a reputation as an up-and-coming manager with superior capabilities. The boss knew him well. However, for the past year he had been on special assignment away from corporate headquarters, so the staffing executive wasn't familiar with him. As it happened, his background and proven experience were particularly suited to the position. In fact, he was so well-suited, he should have been the prime candidate.

This was, in fact, one reason the staffing executive's boss had asked to see the résumés of additional candidates. If this manager was not even included for consideration, he wanted to find out why. If he was included, but not selected, he wanted to see if he was missing some important information before he approved the promotion. The staffing executive was fortunate enough not to overlook forwarding the résumé—then he probably would really have been in trouble. However, had he looked closely at the résumés, he would have immediately realized he was not recommending the best candidate.

In a face-to-face interview with the staffing executive, the boss soon determined that he did not know who should have been the obvious candidate. He could perhaps be forgiven his oversight, but it still did not reflect well on his ability as a high-level manager. Had he promoted the wrong manager, that might have caused a number of problems in the organization. After a discussion of the requirements and the qualifications of the candidates, both the boss and the staffing executive agreed that the formerly ignored candidate should be promoted to the job.

Discuss Your Choice with Colleagues First

I want to state emphatically that Peter Drucker was not saying that a promotion is a group decision. It is not, and you must take responsibility for the outcome, even if those you consult give you erroneous information or possibly a poor recommendation. You are still responsible.

However, it makes sense to share your plans and get others' opinions and ideas whenever it is possible to do so. Had the executive in the example above discussed the appointment with his staff or colleagues, he wouldn't have embarrassed himself in front of his boss. Even if you decide to promote someone whom others don't recommend, at least you'll know the potential pitfalls of your appointment. You'll learn more about what others think and know regarding the various candidates you are considering.

* * *

Once you have made a promotion, your work is not done. You are responsible for what happens next—and there is always "care and feeding" involved. New appointments do not automatically hit the ground running. It's best to prepare the way as much as possible, including thorough training. Sure, you can leave it to the newly promoted employee to work it out by himself or herself. If you've chosen correctly, the individual will know what he or she needs help with or where additional training would be useful. But why wait? There is much you know already that the new appointee probably does not. Unless letting the individual struggle is part of his or her development, why do it? You want your new promotee to be successful and make you look good, don't you?

Without doing everything for the promoted employee, do everything possible to ensure his or her success. As a retired CEO once cautioned his successor about a group of recently promoted vice presidents, "Don't you let them fail!"

CHAPTER THIRTY-EIGHT

Is Leadership a "Marketing Job"?

One of Peter Drucker's far-reaching and integrative ideas isn't well known. This is his belief that good leadership is essentially marketing. People mistake this comment as recommending manipulation, which may be why it is a Drucker concept that is widely ignored. At least, I've never seen it in a leadership book or in a marketing book, except for one of mine. But it was in Drucker's book *Management Challenges for the 21st Century*, which he wrote in 1999, six years before his death. Leadership, Drucker stated, was a "marketing job."[1]

But what was he thinking? Drucker never recommended manipulating subordinates. Quite the contrary. Peter Drucker's view was that all knowledge workers are partners in an organization. As partners, they cannot simply be ordered around and certainly cannot be "managed." They have to be led. This leading involves not only persuasion, which is basic, but also includes an understanding of the goals and objectives of the business, some strategic thinking, and many other elements that we might normally consider part of marketing.

To understand this idea fully, it is important to recognize that Drucker did not say that leadership is "a selling job." He said it is "a marketing job." This is a critical difference. As mentioned in earlier chapters of this book, Drucker explained that selling involves persuading a prospect to buy a product that you want to sell, while marketing is about having a product that a prospect is seeking to buy. Thus, he felt that if marketing is done perfectly, selling is unnecessary.

Why Marketing Isn't Selling

It's fundamental to understand what Drucker believed about selling and marketing before we can relate it to leadership. In Chapters 22 and 34, I explained Drucker's position on marketing. To reiterate, he wrote that not only is marketing not selling, but that the two might not even be complementary. Many marketing experts might take issue with that extraordinary notion, but let's look at marketing first.

Drucker explored the mysteries of marketing, a subject that is second only to leadership in its apparent simplicity yet frequently is even more difficult in its implementation and application. Famed marketing Professor Philip Kotler, who is often referred to as the "Father of Modern Marketing," said, "If I am the Father of Modern Marketing, then Drucker is the Grandfather of Modern Marketing."[2]

In his first book on management, Drucker wrote that there are only two basic functions of business: marketing and innovation. He went on to say that any organization in which marketing is either absent or incidental is not even a business. Thirty-six years later, in a detailed interview with Kotler for inclusion in Drucker's book *Managing the Nonprofit Organization*, Drucker made clear that marketing was not just a concept for business, but for other organizations as well.

What Drucker believed about selling and marketing is the next step in our understanding of this concept. He saw marketing as concerned with top-level thinking, decision making, and strategies. Below this level are various means of carrying out these strategies: advertising, selling, pricing, distribution means, and so on. Many refer to these as lesser strategies useful in the implementation of bigger strategies—they call them "tactics." Like the words *selling* and *marketing*, *tactics* and *strategies* are not the same thing. Strategy is far more im-

portant than tactics. In fact, even when your tactics are less than perfect, if your strategy is the correct one you can still be successful.
That's also what the CEO of Sears Roebuck said about that company's
period of greatest growth. A former military man, General Robert E.
Wood commented, "Business is like war in one respect—if its grand
strategy is correct, any number of tactical errors can be made, and yet
the enterprise proves successful."[3]

Marketing is the higher strategy. Let's look at an example.

Example: Good Tactics, Bad Strategy

Promoted back in 2001, the XFL football league lasted only a single
season. Yet, the guy who thought it up had the experience, know-how,
and past success to present a seemingly sure thing. This was Vince
McMahon, chairman of the World Wrestling Federation. The idea
was to combine the sport of football with pure spectacle, as wrestling
had been combined with spectacle sixty years earlier. McMahon convinced everyone, including NBC, which was a co-sponsor, that he
could duplicate the model of professional wrestling with football and
attain equal success.

McMahon's strategy was to offer this spectacle football as "off-
season football," an additional advantage being that it would not
compete with games played during the regular NFL season. He calculated that it would attract football fans still hungry for the game's
action after the regular season was over. And what football it would
be! Football as it was never seen or imagined before. But he used the
wrong strategy.

The problem was that McMahon's strategy was wrong for the
market segment, which was far from identical to the one for wrestling
audiences. In fact, from the beginning some complained of the
"wrestling feel," which was probably intended as part of the strategy.[4]
Of course, McMahon was ridiculed by mainstream sports journalists,
owing to the "fake" stigma suffered by professional wrestling. However, he expected that, and thought that if anything the "fake" label

would add to XFL's appeal. Even the catchy three letters supported this approach.

Most of McMahon's tactics were actually pretty good. These included good TV coverage (don't forget that NBC was a partner). Then there was the wide-open nature of the football that would be played in the XFL. Football fans relish the hard hits and collisions that define the sport. Yet football injuries have been a concern since the inception of the sport. Even the helmet has been improved to provide additional protection, and strict rules exist against unnecessary roughness. But not in the XFL. There were no penalties for roughness, and there were fewer rules in general. The less strict format was intended to spice things up and contribute to the spectacle: sort of Roman gladiators reborn in modern team competition. The franchises carried names such as Hitmen, Outlaws, and Rage.[5] Only the thumbs-up or thumbs-down of an emperor was missing—and some say that McMahon even thought about this as a possibility.

The players gave it their all, going above and beyond the call of duty. They weren't just a bunch of average Joes hoping to catch on in a professional sports league; many were skilled enough to play in the NFL. And I'm sure the salespeople and those advertising and distributing the tickets did their best. But all of that is *tactics*. The *strategy* was to offer off-season football. But because the strategy was in error, the XFL failed.

Marketing as the Leadership Model

Now let's look at leadership and understand why Drucker asserted that it was "a marketing job." On the face of it, marketing and leadership seem to have little in common. Even the basic development of the two differed greatly. Drucker saw the basic elements of leadership as having been thought through, tried, optimized, and documented in books and known by the ancients millennia ago. Drucker made an oft-repeated comment that the first systematic book on leadership was written by Xenophon 2,500 years ago, and that it was still "the best." Xenophon was a historian and successful Grecian general.

In contrast to leadership, Drucker saw sales and marketing as relatively recent developments. He basically agreed with conventional accounts of the growth of sales, beginning at a time when the first merchants were able to sell a small number of homemade items. For example, think of books. They were originally prepared laboriously by scribes, who frequently spent more time recording the material on sheepskin than the originator did in conceiving the thoughts. A single error could cause the destruction of many weeks of work, since an entire page would need to be redone. To complete a single scroll might take a year or more. Each scroll was unique—there was no such thing as multiple exact copies of a work.

The ancient process was revolutionized in 1450 with the invention of movable type and the printing press, which made multiple copies of printed materials now possible. Further developments in printing and binding eventually enabled books to be available to almost everyone at relatively low cost. So while there was effective leadership in ancient times, there was little need for marketing.

Engineering and technology have been responsible for bringing new products to people's attention. As competition to produce these products increased, eventual overproduction created the need to get rid of this inventory. That's when sales became the issue—being able to sell the product that has been produced. But this, again, is sales, not marketing.

Drucker claimed that it was the Japanese in the seventeenth century who developed the concept of marketing. A merchant came to Tokyo with a revolutionary concept for selling goods. Previously, all selling was done by the manufacturers and farmers themselves, who made or grew what they sold. For the first time, this new merchant didn't sell a single class of goods. He sold all kinds of goods, mostly made by others. He was essentially a buying agent for what his customers wanted. Consequently, this retailer saw his task less as that of persuading others to purchase a product he already owned, and therefore must sell, and instead as that of discovering what his customers wanted and then getting them those products. A successful retailer had to research the market and have ready the products that consumers wanted, or he was soon out of business. This led to research into what the customers wanted and how much they were ready to pay, along with all the other aspects of marketing that have grown up since, including today's emphasis on the buyer and on societal responsibility. The basic idea behind marketing, then, is to have what the customer wants, rather than to try to sell what you have to unsuspecting customers.[6]

An interviewer asked one of the judges on *American Idol* about the overall decline in album sales while at the same time *American Idol* and its alumni had achieved such great success. "That's easy," he said. "The recording studios have been trying to give the public what they think the public wants. We let the public decide, and then we give it to them." The judge's statement reflects pure marketing!

Leadership as an Expression of Marketing

Now let's look at why Drucker asserted that leadership was "a marketing job." On the face of it, marketing and leadership seem to have little in common. Even the basic development of the two fields differs greatly.

Again, Drucker saw the elements of leadership as qualities determined by the ancients millennia ago and optimized over time.

In this view, Drucker stated that it is the leader who is primarily responsible for the organization's future. Therefore, the leader must begin with a mission that he believes in and that is believable to and desired by those he leads. That is a strategic goal. Making the mission believable and communicating and promoting that mission is not only a priority but also a continual process. The leader never ceases to develop and implement the strategies through the use of tactics to reach the goals and objectives that will achieve the organization's mission. That's the nature and process of leadership. And as Peter Drucker concluded in his book regarding our challenges in the new century, that is also the process of marketing. Therefore, leadership is a marketing job.

CHAPTER THIRTY-NINE

You Must Know Your Strengths

Most people think they know their own strengths, but they are almost invariably wrong. This assertion of Peter Drucker's is of critical importance because a person builds great performance on his or her strengths, not by avoiding weaknesses or working to improve areas that are weak. Any individual will always have faults, even the most effective and successful among us. But if you focus on avoiding faults to such an extent that you ignore your strengths and their development, you will be making a major mistake.

History is replete with individuals who made major contributions at critical times, yet had weaknesses that we might wish they did not have. Winston Churchill was a great wartime leader who saved England, and maybe the world, from the Nazis, yet he was known to drink to excess. During the Cuban missile crisis, President John F. Kennedy avoided a nuclear conflagration and war with the Soviet Union, yet he was a womanizer.

General George Patton was a great field general who won more battles with fewer casualties than any other American general during World War II, but he could have a terrible temper when dealing with subordinates. He once slapped a psychologically wounded soldier and called him a coward, which led to Patton's being relieved of command.

Another highly successful general, Douglas MacArthur, has been called swaggering, egotistical, and insubordinate. However, when he was military governor of Japan after World War II, he instituted democracy and won great respect for the United States in a country that was steeped in authoritarian rule. After President Truman fired MacArthur for insubordination, Japanese Prime Minister Shigeru Yoshida declared that MacArthur's accomplishments for Japan were unparalleled and that all Japanese looked upon him with veneration and affection.

While we can work on building our strengths, we are limited by time to do this. So focusing on the development of a minor strength while missing a major one can cause you—in the vernacular—to miss your calling.

Whistler's Other (Ambition)

James Whistler, noted American-born artist of the aesthetic movement whose most famous painting is his portrait *Whistler's Mother,* once wanted to be a soldier. The young Whistler applied to and was accepted to West Point, where he struggled for three years before he finally abandoned his limited talents for what was required at that institution and began to focus on developing the considerable artistic strengths that he possessed. Despite receiving acclaim in the artistic world, he never forgave himself for his failure in a chemistry class for defining a particular solid material as gaseous. He was often heard to lament, "Had silicon been a gas, I would have been a major general."

Whistler was fortunate. While serving as a major general is an important and honorable calling, so is producing great works of art. Even if he had become a major general, he would have been but one of many major generals during the Civil War. Moreover, though Whistler seemed pretty confident of achieving this high rank, the percentage of men from his West Point class who survived battle and competition with others to become major general was less than 5 percent.

Identify Your Strengths

There is only one way to identify your strengths, according to Drucker. He called it "feedback analysis." In a short time, you can identify your strengths—and you'll be surprised. I certainly was. A "short time" for me was maybe two or three days. But Drucker wrote that it would take "only" two or three years! As Lao-tzu, the great Chinese sage, said, "A journey of a thousand miles begins with a single step." Since knowing your strengths is critical, it really doesn't matter how long it takes.

Drucker's methodology for this self-analysis is simple. Every time you must take an important action or make a decision, you write down your expected results. Then, some months later when the results are in, you compare the actual results with your expected results. If the expected and the actual are close, you are competent in this area.[1] If not, continue to do this until you have gained a clear picture of your strengths (and weaknesses). You can also try this with others, such as your subordinates or candidates for a job promotion.

What Do You Do Next?

Drucker suggested that several "action conclusions" should follow your strengths analysis. You know you are strong in certain areas—now what are you going to do about it? In other words, you take action. Drucker identified seven such action conclusions:

1. *Concentrate on your strengths and make them stronger.* Drucker found that strengths are of far more importance than weaknesses. Position yourself so you can use your strengths to produce your very best performance and get optimal results.

I recently read that famed 1930s and '40s actress Hedy Lamarr, born Hedwig Eva Maria Kiesler in Vienna, the only child of assimilated Jewish parents, had a strange background indeed. She made lots of films, but she was most famous for an early film made in Czechoslovakia in 1933, called *Ecstasy*. Need I say more? In a time when appearing in a bikini would have been cause for arrest, Lamarr was in a movie that included frontal nudity and a simulated orgasm, the realism for which was achieved by the director's jabbing her in the buttocks with a safety pin. However, Lamarr was also a math prodigy and was co-inventor of the wireless technology used in Bluetooth and cell phones today. She made thirty-two films; none spectacular, yet the technology she invented was truly remarkable and has had widespread impact on our world of today. Only she would be able to answer the question of whether or not she chose wisely in her career.

2. *Work on improving your strengths.* Steve Jobs didn't invent an industry by turning his computer skills into party games. He kept improving them throughout his lifetime; he introduced the iPad less than two years before his death. Alfred von Schlieffen had a strategic plan for Germany's winning World War I in a two-front war. It is said that von Schlieffen's final words were, "Keep the right wing strong." Alas, his successors failed to follow these final instructions, and Germany lost the war.

3. *Identify where intellectual arrogance causes disabling ignorance.* Now, what is Drucker talking about? He says that this third point is of particular importance. That's because he's talking about a situation in which you have overwhelming knowledge in one area that causes you to neglect the knowledge in other areas to the extent of almost complete ignorance. A friend of mine who dealt regularly with a number of highly educated people, some of whom were contemptuous of anyone less educated than they were, used to call such snobs "educated idiots." Drucker would have agreed. He said that such people frequently demonstrate poor performance owing to concentrated knowledge in too narrow a field.

4. *Remedy your shortcomings or bad habits.* Don't ignore your short-comings or bad habits using the excuse that you're developing your strengths. If a weakness affects your major strength that you are developing, you have a problem and must fix it.

5. *Demonstrate good manners.* How many bright, knowledgeable people fail because they lack the necessary social graces? Drucker called manners the "lubricating oil" of an organization.

6. *Don't take on assignments in which you are incompetent.* Don't agree to be a Chinese interpreter unless you speak and understand Chinese. Pretty obvious, huh? Yet, haven't you seen someone volunteer to carve the Thanksgiving turkey even though he or she hasn't a clue what to do and leaves behind a butchered mess?

7. *Don't waste a lot of time raising your performance in weak areas.* Drucker stressed that your time should be spent on raising your high skills and competence levels to even higher levels.

Other Important Qualities to Consider

Building on Drucker's concept of staffing for strength, I think there are other qualities you must consider in addition to your strengths. These include what you like to do, what you think you should do, and what you want to do. If you are doing the staffing for your organization, and are responsible for placing round pegs in round holes, you need to consider your staff's strengths, as well as what you would like them to do, what you think they should do, and what you want them to do.

For example, you may have two Russian interpreters of equal ability, but there's only one position available. Or, there may be a personality clash that requires an individual to be placed in a certain job and not in another. To blindly staff without considering all aspects of the individuals involved and the environment in which they will function would be foolish. However, all considerations of strengths and weaknesses start with a knowledge of strengths, yours and those you work with.

CHAPTER FORTY

Drucker's Most Valuable Lesson

Journalists who interview me about my books on Drucker frequently ask me: What was Drucker's most valuable lesson? With Drucker's so many insights, so many wonderful ideas, so much ethical and moral guidance that might have saved organizations or even countries from financial ruin, I find this an almost impossible question to answer. For several years, my response was something along the lines of, "It all depends." I pointed out that Drucker's "most valuable lesson" was situational—that it depends primarily on what issue someone is considering. I avoided naming a single lesson that covers all instances because I couldn't think of one lesson that overshadowed all the others.

Recently, I rethought this matter, however, and I decided I could do a lot better. I reviewed various Drucker prescriptions for a range of problem areas. Was there a thread of commonality in his predictions? Some recommendations and solutions that might lead to a universal lesson? A principle that might honestly be entitled "Most Valuable"?

Do the Right Thing

If it was an ethical issue, Drucker might recommend, "Do the right thing, and since the definition of 'the right thing' is based on so many situational and cultural factors, above all, think it through to ensure that, above all, you do no harm."

In the Los Angeles area where I live, the small town of Bell (population 40,000) came under national scrutiny in 2010, when it was discovered that the city manager had an annual salary of nearly $800,000. Other top executives were being similarly rewarded. Even city council members had salaries of over $100,000 a year for their part-time positions, which involved meetings lasting only a few minutes each month. All this while employees in that same city government, some in essential services and others making $9 an hour, were being laid off owing to "budget cutbacks" and the recession. This was not even a wealthy town. It was and is a working-class town. That this situation was wrong was obvious to all.

Drucker died in 2005. However, he knew forty years ago that extremely high CEO salaries were unethical. Why would any CEO need to make 300 times that earned by the lowest-level employee—when the ratio of highest-paid to lowest-paid employee in every other country in the world was no more than 20 to 1? Drucker said that this imbalance caused immeasurable harm—to the company, to the industry, and to society—and he advised stopping the practice.

But advocates claimed that these incredibly high salaries were necessary to attract the best talent. They asserted further that these huge compensations were justified by the wealth these well-heeled executives created for the organizations. But Drucker pointed out that these giant bankrolls were paid whether the company was making or losing money. A few executives chose to limit their own salaries; most did not. Drucker predicted that we would eventually pay a terrible price for this lapse in fairness. Many top executives never forgave him for publicizing the matter, and many of us didn't even think much about it until the onset of the Great Recession that began in 2008.

Find Out What the Customer Values

If a matter was a marketing challenge, Drucker would advise us to think it through to determine what the customer considered of value and to be extremely cautious that marketers didn't substitute their own definitions of value for those of the customers or prospects. This is a valuable insight. If you go down a list of failed products, you will find at their core this marketing problem; even geniuses are not immune.

A young Steven Jobs claimed that the Lisa computer would be successful because it was so superior technologically to any of its competitors. The Lisa had an advanced system-protected memory, multitasking ability, a sophisticated operating system, a built-in screensaver, an advanced calculator, support for up to two megabytes (MB) of RAM, expansion slots, a numeric keypad, data corruption protection, a larger and higher-resolution screen display, and more. It would be years before many of those features were implemented in any other computer. Still, Jobs was wrong. All of these features resulted in Lisa's high price of about $22,000 in today's dollars, and so buyers opted for the far less expensive, although technologically inferior, IBM at less than a third of Lisa's cost. Apple's prospects valued cost above technological superiority at the time.

Promotion and Placement of People

Drucker had a number of good ideas regarding placement and promotion decisions. For instance, if you put a previously successful employee in a job in which he fails, that failure is yours—the manager who put the individual in the job—not the proven employee who was given the assignment. As a corollary, Drucker abhorred the idea so popular in many organizations of "the whole man concept." That is, you look for individuals who are well-rounded, minimally acceptable in all facets of their managerial responsibilities but superior in none. He emphasized that at best you'll end up with an organization staffed with individuals who are wonderfully adequate, but none who are the best in an assigned role. Ironically, he pointed to the military (ironic because for years the military had been promoting "the whole man concept"), and he chose to compare two generals: George Patton (an example I've mentioned earlier in this book) and Dwight Eisenhower.

George Patton could motivate his soldiers to extraordinary efforts. He could accomplish any mission on the battlefield and do this with one of the lowest battlefield casualty rates of any senior commander. However, Patton couldn't get along with his allies. He said, and sometimes did, things that were certain to get him into trouble. In contrast, Eisenhower had never even fought on a battlefield and would have been totally lost in Patton's job. But he knew how to get senior officers from many different backgrounds and cultures to work together and how to minimize their differences and squabbles. He was the best choice for Supreme Allied Commander in Europe, just as Patton was the best choice for commanding an army group in the field.

Drucker's solution? Think it through and staff for strength. Ensure that weaknesses, whatever they are, are irrelevant for a particular assignment.

Think for Ourselves

I thought a lot about Drucker's various solutions to different problems. It seemed to me that what Peter Drucker was doing was asking us to think. He did not accept "common knowledge" or the way things were being done as necessarily being correct. In fact, the phrase I heard him use most in the classroom was "What everybody knows is usually wrong."

Drucker never claimed great knowledge about anything, especially in his legendary consulting. Instead, he claimed great ignorance, which required him to think and ask questions. Chapter 35 relates the story he used to prove this point. In brief, because the British were losing too many transport ships to German submarines during World War II, they developed a basic design to build replacement ships more cheaply. British shipbuilders were considered the best in the world, but Britain was engaged in fighting the war and lacked the manpower, shipyards, and production facilities to build the fleet. Out of desperation the British turned to the United States for help, even though we did not have much shipbuilding capacity. American industrialist Henry Kaiser came to the rescue, even though he knew little or nothing about shipbuilding. Approaching the problem from the stance of ignorance, Kaiser revolutionized the operation and ended up producing the ships even faster and more efficiently than had the British.

The Tortoise and the Hare

The Sydney to Melbourne Ultra Marathon was held in the years between 1981 and 1993 and was regarded as the toughest footrace in the world. It was 544 miles long and took up to seven days to complete, with stops for rest permitted along the way. Most athletes ran all day and rested at night. In 1983, an unknown sixty-one-year-old potato farmer by the name of Cliff Young entered the race. Many thought he would be lucky to finish. But Young didn't accept what everyone knew to be true or follow the way things had always been done. He thought about the race, not from experience and expertise but from complete ignorance. He realized that he could walk the distance if he chose to and that he wasn't required to stop overnight. So he didn't. Result? He won, shaving almost two days off the previous record and finishing almost a day ahead of the second-place winner, who was half his age.

* * *

What was Drucker's most valuable lesson? He taught us to think and ask questions.

ENDNOTES

Chapter One

1. Peter F. Drucker, *The Changing World of the Executive* (New York: Harper & Row, 1982), p. 245.

2. Peter F. Drucker, *Management: Tasks, Responsibilities, Practices* (New York: Harper & Row, 1973), p. 367.

3. Drucker, *Changing World*, p. 245.

4. Ibid.

5. Peter F. Drucker and Joseph A. Maciariello, *The Daily Drucker* (New York: Harper Business, 2004), p. 126.

6. Ibid.

7. Ibid.

8. Ibid., pp. 248–54.

9. N. S. Gill, "Is 'First Do No Harm' from the Hippocratic Oath? Myth vs. Fact," *About.com*, accessed January 23, 2013, http://ancienthistory.about.com/od/greekmedicine/f/HippocraticOath.htm.

10. Peter F. Drucker, *Management Challenges for the 21st Century* (New York: Harper Business, 1999), pp. 175–76.

Chapter Two

1. Ralph L. Sheets, "Frank L. Schmidt, PhD," *Gallup*, accessed January 21, 2014, http://www.gallup.com/corporate/22657/Frank-Schmidt-PhD.aspx.

2. Peter F. Drucker, *The Practice of Management* (New York: Harper & Brothers, 1954), pp. 302–303.

3. Ibid., p. 304.

4. Charles Garfield, *Peak Performers: The New Heroes of American Business* (New York: Avon, 1986), p. 26.

5. Drucker, *Practice of Management*, p. 305.

6. Ibid., pp. 306–307.

Chapter Three

1. This chapter is adapted from my "Leadership Laws: It Was Drucker's Favorite Book," *Leadership Excellence*, January 16, 2009. [A shorter version of this article, "Peter Drucker's Favorite Leadership Book," appeared in my column *Lessons from Peter Drucker*, Human Resources, IQ and their affiliates, http://www.humanresourcesiq.com/drucker-on-management/columns/peter-drucker-s-favorite-leadership-bo and my *Drucker on Leadership* (San Francisco: Jossey-Bass, 2010), pp. 121–31.]

2. Peter F. Drucker, *The Practice of Management* (New York: Harper & Brothers, 1954), p. 194.

3. Ibid.

4. Xenophon, *The Persian Expedition*, trans. Rex Warner (Baltimore: Penguin, 1949), p. 99.

5. Ibid., p. 103.

6. Ibid., p. 124.

7. Ibid., p. 108.

8. Xenophon, *The Education of Cyrus*, trans. Wayne Ambler (Ithaca, NY: Cornell University Press, 2001), pp. 52–53.

Chapter Four

1. "The Seven Deadly Sins," *White Stone Journal.com*, June 18, 1996, with update March 20, 2008, accessed January 25, 2012, http://www.white stonejournal.com/seven_deadly_sins.

2. Kitta MacPherson, "Petraeus Challenges Seniors to Pursue Life of Public Service," *News at Princeton*, May 31, 2009, accessed March 5, 2013, http://www.princeton.edu/main/news/archive/S24/38/10A46.

3. Randy "Duke" Cunningham, media release statement, O'Melveny & Myers LLP, November 28, 2005, accessed January 25, 2012, http://www.signonsandiego.com/news/politics/cunningham/images/051128cunningham_resign.pdf.

4. Peter F. Drucker, "The American CEO," *Wall Street Journal*, December 30, 2004, accessed June 2, 2008, http://online.wsj.com/article/SB113207479926289 7747.html.

5. Kenneth Blanchard and Spencer Johnson, *The One-Minute Manager* (New York: William Morrow, 1982), p. 53.

6. Jeanne Sahadi, "CEO Pay," *CNN: Money*, accessed January 25, 2013, http://money.cnn.com/2005/08/26/news/economy/ceo_pay.

7. John A. Byrne, "The Man Who Invented Management," *BusinessWeek*, November 28, 2005, accessed January 25, 2013, http://businessweek.com/magazine/content/05_48/b3961001.htm.

Chapter Five

1. Peter F. Drucker, "Managing the Increasing Complexity of Large Organizations," in *The Drucker Lectures*, edited by Rick Wartzman (New York: McGraw-Hill, 2010), p. 87.

Chapter Six

1. Max DePree, *Leadership Is an Art* (New York: Dell, 1989).

2. James MacGregor Burns, as quoted in *Leadership* by William Safire and Leonard Safir (New York: Simon & Schuster, 1990), p. 202.

3. Connie Podesta and Jean Gatz, *How to Be the Person Successful Companies Fight to Keep* (New York: Simon & Schuster, 1997), p. 184.

4. Bob Nelson, *1501 Ways to Reward Employees* (New York: Workman, 2012).

Chapter Eight

1. James MacGregor Burns, as quoted in *Leadership* by William Safire and Leonard Safir (New York: Simon & Schuster, 1990), p. 4.

2. Ibid., p. 244.

3. Peter F. Drucker, *Management, Tasks, Responsibilities, Practices* (New York: Harper & Row, 1973), p. 232.

4. "Douglas McGregor," Yale University Library database, accessed March 5, 2013, http://yufind.library.yale.edu/yufind/Author/Home?author= McGregor,%20Douglas.

5. Peter F. Drucker, *The Practice of Management* (New York: Harper & Brothers, 1954), p. 159. See also William A. Cohen, *Drucker on Leadership* (San Francisco: Jossey-Bass, 2010), pp. 121–31.

6. *FM-6-0 Mission Command: Command and Control of Army Forces* (Washington, DC: U.S. Government Printing Office, 2003), accessed March 5, 2013, http://www.globalsecurity.org/military/library/policy/army/fm/6-0/chap1.htm.

Chapter Nine

1. "Immaculate Conception," Catholic Encyclopedia, accessed January 29, 2013, http://www.newadvent.org/cathen/07674d.htm.

2. Jerry Knight, "Tylenol's Maker Shows How to Respond to Crisis," *Washington Post*, October 11, 1982; also referenced in Tamara Kaplan, "The Tylenol Crisis," accessed January 29, 2013, http://www.aerobiologic alengineering.com/wxk116/TylenolMurders/crisis.html.

Chapter Ten

1. Eric Basu, "Doing the Right Thing—When People Are Watching, but Don't Care," *Forbes*, April 23, 2012, accessed January 30, 2013, http://www.forbes.com/sites/ericbasu/2012/04/23/doing-the-right-thing-when-people-are-watching-but-dont-care.

Chapter Eleven

1. "Failure to Success Stories," *Want to Know.Info*, accessed March 6, 2013, http://www.wanttoknow.info/060520inspirationalstories.

2. Peter Hart, "From Gallipoli to D-Day," *BBC History*, accessed January 31, 2013, http://www.bbc.co.uk/history/worldwars/wwtwo/gallipoli_dday_01.shtml.

Chapter Thirteen

1. "The Drucker Perspective," editorial, *PEX ProcessExcellence Network*, September 19, 2011, accessed February 2, 2013, http://www.process excellencenetwork.com/people-performance-and-change-in-process-improveme/columns/the-secret-to-achieving-more-with-less-increasin.

2. Peter F. Drucker, "*Really* Reinventing Government," *Atlantic Monthly*, February 1995, accessed February 2, 2013, http://www.theatlantic.com/past/politics/polibig/reallyre.htm.

Chapter Fifteen

1. "Primum non Nocere," *Wesley's Medical Page*, accessed February 3, 2013, http://www.eastridges.com/wesley/primum.html.

2. "Enron Scandal at a Glance," *BBC News World Edition*, August 22, 2002, accessed February 5, 2013, http://news.bbc.co.uk/2/hi/business/1780075.stm.

3. Vlasenko, Polina, "How Did We Get into This Mess? The Origins of the Housing Crisis," *American Institute for Economic Research*, September 21, 2008, accessed January 1, 2009, http://www.aier.org/research/commentaries/554-how-did-we-get-into-this-mess-the-origins-of-the-housing-crisis.

4. "The Fuel That Fed the Subprime Meltdown," *Investopedia*, February 6, 2009, accessed February 5, 2013, http://www.investopedia.com/articles/07/subprime-overview.asp#axzz2K4WQMcaY.

5. "Subprime Mortgage Crisis," Wikipedia entry, accessed February 3, 2013, http://en.wikipedia.org/wiki/Subprime_mortgage_crisis.

Chapter Seventeen

1. Peter F. Drucker, *The Essential Drucker* (New York: HarperCollins, 2001), p. 172.

2. Peter F. Drucker, *Management Challenges for the 21st Century* (New York: HarperCollins, 1999), p. 146.

3. Peter F. Drucker, *Managing for the Future* (New York: Truman Talley/ Dutton, 1992), p. 104.

Chapter Eighteen

1. Gwendolyn Vines Gettliffe, "How Were We Able to Navigate from the Earth to the Moon with Such Precision?" *MIT Engineering: Ask an Engineer*, accessed February 7, 2013, http://engineering.mit.edu/live/news/1909-how-were-we-able-to-navigate-from-the-earth-to-the.

2. Peter F. Drucker, *Management: Tasks, Responsibilities, Practices* (New York: Harper & Row, 1973), p. 496.

3. Ibid.

4. "Hawthorne Effect," *Psychology Wiki*, accessed March 10, 2013, http://psychology.wikia.com/wiki/Hawthorne_effect.

5. Jay Mathews and Peter Katel, "The Cost of Quality," *Newsweek*, September 7, 1992, p. 48.

6. Drucker, *Management: Tasks*, p. 497.

Chapter Nineteen

1. Kimberly McCall, "Crash and Learn," *Entrepreneur.com*, October 1, 2000, accessed February 9, 2013, http://www.entrepreneur.com/article/32078#.

2. "Zapmail and Satellite Systems: The Zapmail Project," *FedEx Legends*, May 30, 2011, accessed February 9, 2013, http://www.fedexlegends.info/zapmail/zapmail.html.

3. "Zapmail," *Wikipedia*, accessed February 9, 2013, http://en.wikipedia.org/wiki/Zapmail.

4. "The Expansion of Pre-K Education: The Right Solution at the Wrong Time?" New Jersey School Boards Association, accessed March 10, 2013, http://www.njsba.org/blog/?p=106.

Chapter Twenty

1. Doris Drucker, *Invent Radium or I'll Pull Your Hair* (Chicago: University of Chicago Press, 2004).

2. Peter F. Drucker, "The Information That Executives Truly Need," *Harvard Business Review* 73 (January 1995), p. 54.

Chapter Twenty-One

1. John A. Byrne, "The Man Who Invented Management," *BusinessWeek*, November 28, 2005, accessed February 12, 2013, http://businessweek.com/magazine/content/05_48/b3961001.htm.

Chapter Twenty-Two

1. Conversation with the author, Palm Springs, California, April 27, 1984.

2. Robert E. Wood, quoted in *Strategy and Structure* by A. D. Chandler Jr. (Cambridge, MA: MIT Press, 1962), p. 235.

3. Carol D. Leonnig and Joe Stephens, "Lawmakers Accuse Solyndra Execs of Ripping Off Taxpayers," *Washington Post Politics*, accessed February 13, 2013, http://www.washingtonpost.com/blogs/2chambers/post/solyndra-executives-to-appear-before-house-committee-friday-morning/2011/09/22/gIQAF0vCqK_blog.html.

4. "Great Lessons from the Great Depression," *CPIFinancial.net*, August 10, 2009, accessed February 13, 2013, http://www.cpifinancial.net/features/post/11273/great-lessons-from-the-great-depression.

5. "Successful Companies and Industries During the Great Depression," *Google Answers*, accessed February 13, 2013, http://answers.google.com/answers/threadview?id=178334.

6. "P&G Sponsors Its First Daytime Serial," *Old Time.com*, accessed February 13, 2013, http://www.old-time.com/commercials/1930%27s/OOMP.htm.

Chapter Twenty-Three

1. Peter F. Drucker, "Drucker on Management: The Five Deadly Business Sins," *Wall Street Journal*, October 21, 1993, p. A18.
2. Ibid.
3. Peter F. Drucker, *Managing for the Future* (New York: Truman Talley/Dutton, 1992), pp. 251–52.
4. Ibid.
5. Drucker, "Drucker on Management."

Chapter Twenty-Four

1. For a full discussion of these principles and their development, see William A. Cohen, *The Art of the Strategist* (New York: AMACOM, 2004), pp. 3–109.
2. "Langley Aerodrome," *Wikipedia*, accessed March 16, 2013, http://en.wikipedia.org/wiki/Langley_Aerodrome.

Chapter Twenty-Five

1. Peter A. Drucker, *Innovation and Entrepreneurship* (New York: Harper & Row, 1985).
2. William A. Cohen, "The Entrepreneurial Drucker," *Business Forum* 11 (Winter 1986), pp. 26–27.
3. "Starbucks," *Wikipedia*, accessed February 15, 2013, http://en.wikipedia.org/wiki/Starbucks.
4. "Keurig," *Wikipedia*, accessed February 15, 2013, http://en.wikipedia.org/wiki/Keurig.

5. Jane Marchiony Paretti, "The Man Who Invented the Ice Cream Cone," *Hudson Reporter.com*, September 14, 2005, accessed February 15, 2013, http://www.hudsonreporter.com/view/full_story/2405732/article-The-man-who-invented-the-ice-cream-cone-Italo-Marchiony-created-the-dish-you-could-eat---and-he-created-it-in-Hoboken.

Chapter Twenty-Six

1. Peter F. Drucker, *The Essential Drucker* (New York: HarperCollins, 2001), p. 146.

2. Peter F. Drucker, *Management Challenges for the 21st Century* (New York: Harper Business, 1999), p. 87.

3. Kevin Eikenberry, "When Stressed . . . ." *Leadership and Learning,* accessed June 9, 2013, http://blog.kevineikenberry.com/leadership/when-stressed.

4. Louis E. Grivettit, "Dialog: Recent Vietnam Stories Since the War," accessed February 15, 2013, http://www.pbs.org/pov/stories/vietnam/bios/grivetti.html.

5. Peter F. Drucker, *Managing the Non-Profit Organization* (New York: HarperCollins, 1990), p. 100.

Chapter Twenty-Seven

1. Peter F. Drucker, *Managing for the Future* (New York: Truman Talley/Dutton, 1992), p. 251.

2. Ibid., p. 252.

3. Douglas MacArthur, *Reminiscences* (New York: McGraw-Hill, 1964), p. 70.

Chapter Twenty-Eight

1. Peter F. Drucker, *Management: Tasks, Responsibilities, Practices* (New York: Harper & Row, 1973), p. 65.

2. Peter F. Drucker, *The Essential Drucker* (New York: Harper Business, 2001), p. 183.

3. Peter F. Drucker, *Management Challenges for the 21st Century* (New York: Harper Business, 1999), p. 115.

4. Ibid., p. 114.

Chapter Thirty

1. Thomas F. Mulligan and James Flanigan, "Prolific Father of Modern Management," *Los Angeles Times*, November 12, 2005, p. A-1, accessed February 19, 2013, http://articles.latimes.com/2005/nov/12/business/fi-drucker12.

2. Robert Heller, "The Drucker Legacy," *Thinking Managers*, accessed February 19, 2013, http://www.thinkingmanagers.com/management/drucker.

3. Peter F. Drucker, *Managing for Results* (New York: Harper & Row, 1964), pp. 143–46.

4. Peter F. Drucker, *On the Profession of Management* (Boston: Harvard Business Review Book, 1998), pp. 116–17.

5. Drucker, *Managing for Results*, p. 221.

6. "'Neutron Jack' Exits," *New York Times*, September 9, 2001, accessed June 13, 2013, http://www.nytimes.com/2001/09/09/opinion/neutron-jack-exits.htm.

7. Peter F. Drucker, "*Really* Reinventing Government," *Atlantic Monthly*, February 1995, accessed June 9, 2013, http://www.theatlantic.com/past/politics/polibig/reallyre.htm.

8. Peter F. Drucker, with Joseph Maciariello, *Management*, rev. ed. (New York: HarperCollins, 2008), pp. 163–66.

9. Drucker, *Managing for Results*, p. 143.

10. Ibid., p. 144.

11. Peter F. Drucker, *Innovation and Entrepreneurship* (New York: Harper & Row, 1985), p. 155.

12. Drucker and Maciariello, *Management*, p. 61.

13. Drucker, *Managing for Results*, pp. 144–45.

14. Peter F. Drucker, *Management Challenges for the 21st Century* (New York: Harper Business, 1999), pp. 74–76.

15. Drucker, *On the Profession of Management*, pp. 25–26.

Chapter Thirty-One

1. Peter F. Drucker, *Innovation and Entrepreneurship* (New York: Harper & Row, 1985), p. 36.

2. Steven Kates, "Supply Creates Its Own Demand," *History of Economic Review*, accessed March 5, 2013, http://www.hetsa.org/pdf/41-A-3.pdf.

3. "Silly Putty," *Inventor of the Week*, accessed March 5, 2013, http://web.mit.edu/invent/iow/sillyputty.html.

4. Peter F. Drucker, *Managing for Results* (New York: Harper & Row, 1964), pp. 147–48.

Chapter Thirty-Two

1. Peter F. Drucker, *Management: Tasks, Responsibilities, Practices* (New York: Harper & Row, 1973), p. 60.

2. Ibid.

3. "Profit Motive," *Investopedia*, accessed March 6, 2013, http://www.investopedia.com/terms/p/profit-motive.asp#axzz2MmHOFrFf.

4. "Profit Motive," *Wikipedia*, accessed March 6, 2013, http://en.wikipedia.org/wiki/Profit_motive.

5. "10 Highly-Rated Charities with Low Paid CEOs," *Charity Navigator*, accessed March 6, 2013, http://www.charitynavigator.org/index.cfm?bay=topten.detail&listid=92.

6. Drucker, *Management: Tasks, Responsibilities, Practices*, p. 61.

Chapter Thirty-Three

1. Peter F. Drucker, "The New Meaning of Corporate Responsibility," *California Management Review* 26, no. 2 (Winter 1984), p. 56.

2. Ibid., p. 62.

3. William A. Cohen, *A Class with Drucker* (New York: AMACOM, 2008), p. 120.

4. "Julius Rosenwald," *Wikipedia*, accessed March 7, 2013, http://en. wikipedia.org/wiki/Julius_Rosenwald.

5. David A. Thomas, "IBM Finds Profit in Diversity," *Working Knowledge*, Harvard Business School Newsletter, September 27, 2004, accessed March 7, 2013, http://hbswk.hbs.edu/item/4389.html.

Chapter Thirty-Four

1. Peter F. Drucker, *The Practice of Management* (New York: HarperCollins, 1986), p. 37.

2. Peter F. Drucker, *Management: Tasks, Responsibilities, Practices* (New York: Harper & Row, 1973), p. 61.

3. Marvin Thomas, "The Burma Shave Phenomenon," Montgomery College website, accessed March 8, 2013, http://www.montgomery college.edu/Departments/hpolscrv/mthomas.htm.

4. Martin Waterman, "Feeling Nostalgic? Now You'll Rave! Here's the Story of Burma Shave," *Backwoods Home Magazine*, accessed March 8, 2013, http://www.backwoodshome.com/articles/waterman37.html.

5. *Burma-Shave.org*, accessed March 8, 2013, http://burma-shave.org/.

Chapter Thirty-Five

1. John H. Lienhard, "No. 1525: Liberty Ships," *Engines of Our Ingenuity*, accessed March 11, 2013, http://www.uh.edu/engines/epi1525.htm.

Chapter Thirty-Six

1. Elizabeth H. Edersheim, *The Definitive Drucker* (New York: McGraw-Hill, 2007), p. 17.

2. Bernard Law (Viscount Montgomery of Alamein), *The Memoirs of Field-Marshal The Viscount Montgomery of Alamein, K.G.* (New York: World, 1958), p. 94.

Chapter Thirty-Seven

1. Peter F. Drucker, *On the Profession of Management* (Boston: Harvard Business School Press, 1998), p. 40.

2. "The Academy Commitment," U.S. Air Force Academy website, accessed March 18, 2013, http://www.academyadmissions.com/commitment.

3. Peter F. Drucker, *The Effective Executive* (New York: HarperCollins, 2004), pp. 78–92. In a chapter entitled "Staffing for Excellence," in his book *People and Performance* (New York: Harper College, 1977), Drucker discusses three rules for effective staffing. However, by the time his updated version of the *Effective Executive* appeared in 2004, this list had grown to four rules, the fourth being a cautionary one about staffing for the single strength that was most needed and being wary of staffing primarily for well-rounded leaders. I discussed this before introducing the three rules.

Chapter Thirty-Eight

1. Peter F. Drucker, *Management Challenges for the 21st Century* (New York: Harper Business, 1999), p. 21.

2. Philip Kotler, quoted in my *Drucker on Marketing* (New York: McGraw-Hill, 2013), p. vii.

3. Robert E. Wood, quoted in *Strategy and Structure* by A. D. Chandler Jr. (Cambridge, MA: MIT Press, 1962), p. 235.

4. *XFL—The History*, accessed March 28, 2013, http://www.rememberthexfl.8m.com/history.html.

5. "XFL," *Wikipedia,* accessed March 28, 2013, http://en.wikipedia.org/wiki/XFL.

6. Peter F. Drucker, *Management: Tasks, Responsibilities, Practices* (New York: Harper & Row, 1974), p. 62.

Chapter Thirty-Nine

1. Peter F. Drucker, *The Essential Drucker* (New York: Harper Business, 2001), p. 218.

INDEX

tasks, accurate definitions of, 107
technologies
   changes in, 99, 100
   introducing, 123
   and obsolescence of products, 120
Temple, Shirley, 122
Theory X, 51
Theory Y, 51, 52
thinking
   encouraging workers in, 42–43
   in job searches, 79
   prior to abandonment, 190–191
   for yourself, 253–254
timing, 117–124, 158
toll-gate position, 162
total profit, 147
Total Quality Management (TQM),
   113–114
transactional leadership, 50
transformational leadership, 50, 52
trends, 127
Truman, Harry, on Senate Committees,
   10
Tuskegee Airmen, 213
Tuskegee Institute, 213
Tylenol, 59–60

the unexpected
   doing, 157
   as richest source of innovation,
     184–187
   in supply-side innovation, 194
unintended consequences, 92–96, 212
Union Pacific railroad, 99
Universidad del Rosario (Bogotá,
   Colombia), 1
unlimited liability clause, 211–212
U.S. Air Force Academy, 234
U.S. Post Office, 164
utils, 163, 164

value
   from customer"s perspective, 146,
     168–169, 177–182, 252

in ignorance, 221–225
from manufacturer"s perspective, 146
quality as part of, 104
Vandenberg, Hoyt S., 34
vision, managerial, 18–19
the Vital Few, Rule of, 82
Volkswagen, 129
volunteerism, 35–36, 39, 40, 203
von Schlieffen, Alfred, 248

Wallace Company, 113
Wall Street (movie), 201
Walmart, 211–212
Walton, Sam, 211–212
Washington, George, 35
Washington Mutual, 98
water-saving toilets, 94
Watson, Thomas, 69
Webern, Anton, 33
Welch, Jack, 34, 83, 156, 188–190, 193,
   234
Welles, Carson, on Anton Chigurh, 8
Whistler, James, 246
Whistler, Thomas, 17
"whole man concept," 252
wisdom, 55–60
The Wizard of Oz (movie), 122
Wood, Robert E., on business, 141, 240
Wozniak, Steve, 166
Wright brothers, 119, 156, 166

Xenophon, 21–26, 52–53, 242
Xerox, 146–147
XFL football league, 240–241

York, Alvin C., 45–46
Yoshida, Shigeru, 246
Young, Cliff, 254

Zapmail, 120
Zipf, George K., 82